Mrs. Brown's A-Zy of Everything

Mrs. Brown's
A–Zy
of Everything

By Agnes Brown
with Brendan O'Carroll
and Michael Joseph

MICHAEL JOSEPH

Published by the Penguin Group
Penguin Books Ltd, 80 Strand, London WC2R 0RL, England
Penguin Group (USA) Inc., 375 Hudson Street, New York, New York 10014, USA
Penguin Group (Canada), 90 Eglinton Avenue East, Suite 700, Toronto, Ontario, Canada M4P 2Y3
(a division of Pearson Penguin Canada Inc.)
Penguin Ireland, 25 St Stephen's Green, Dublin 2, Ireland
(a division of Penguin Books Ltd)
Penguin Group (Australia), 707 Collins Street, Melbourne, Victoria 3008, Australia
(a division of Pearson Australia Group Pty Ltd)
Penguin Books India Pvt Ltd, 11 Community Centre,
Panchsheel Park, New Delhi – 110 017, India
Penguin Group (NZ), 67 Apollo Drive, Rosedale, North Shore 0632, New Zealand
(a division of Pearson New Zealand Ltd)
Penguin Books (South Africa) (Pty) Ltd, Block D, Rosebank Office Park,
181 Jan Smuts Avenue, Parktown North, Gauteng 2193, South Africa

Penguin Books Ltd, Registered Offices: 80 Strand, London WC2R 0RL, England

www.penguin.com

First published 2014
001

Text copyright © Brendan O'Carroll, Jason Hazeley and Joel Morris, 2014
Design copyright © Unreal Ltd, 2014
All photographs copyright © Bocpix Ltd, 2014
Additional images from Dorling Kindersley and Shutterstock

Printed and bound in Italy by Printer Trento Srl
Colour reproduction by Altaimage, London

A CIP catalogue record for this book is available from the British Library

ISBN: 978-0-718-17895-6

This book is dedicated to the wit and humour of Michael Gibney and firefighters everywhere.

CONTENTS

INTRODUCTION

Hello there!

Ginger Balls was so delighted with all the useful information I gave him in my last book that he asked me to put together another.

I was delighted as I so want to write *The History of Laundry and Ironing*. When I suggested this he said no. He said he wanted something more general, more modern: he said he didn't want to be disappointed again. (He met his wife on Facebook and she looks nothing like her profile picture.)

So welcome to my newest guide to living the Mrs Brown lifestyle. This a response to the many people (actually two) who were so delighted with the *Family Handbook* that they are now asking me for more advice on life itself.

Life is actually quite simple. Get up in the morning, do what you have to do, go back to bed at night.

My mother used to say, 'It's only the hair on a gooseberry that stops it from being a grape,' — I still haven't a clue what she was talking about.

But I do have 'life' experience; well as the mother of a bag load of kids (one forceps) it is impossible not to gain some life experience. One thing I have learned is that all my children are different. You must love and cherish them all in an individual way. If you are at this point in your life raising teenagers, you have my sympathy. It WILL pass but I know exactly what you are going through right now — it is only when your children become teenagers that you can understand why some animals eat their young!

Enjoy the book, and keep Ginger Balls happy and in a job.

Much love,

Agnes Brown

Agnes Loretta Brown
Dublin, 2014

Aa

... is for 'Abroad' among other things

ABROAD

You can say what you like about Abroad, but it's not feckin' home. And the weather's never the same. It's either so hot you're sweating like a sauna worker's cheese sandwich, or you're huddling up to the penguins to stop yourself from freezing to death.

Plus there's the rain. In some of these places it starts raining and doesn't stop for three months. Like Europe.

And then there's the wildlife. Spiders that can kill you. Trees that can poison you if you so much as look at them. Feckin' snakes. Whoever designed the snake was a bloody maniac. 'Worms. They're not nice. Right so. I'll make giant ones. Giant worms that make a noise like a gas leak. Giant worms that can either wring your neck or swallow you whole. And you can't see them coming. Is that scary enough?' Might as well have made them invisible, and drunk, and given them a shotgun. God knows the ghost of a snake must be the scariest feckin' thing known to mankind.

When you go abroad, it's best to take some basics with you. Like tinned food. Our Trevor had to eat some frightening rubbish on his travels: grasshoppers, brains, miniature rice. I offered to send him a suitcase full of baked beans, but he said, 'Mammy, when in Rome…' So I sent him a suitcase full of feckin' pizza.

So where to go abroad? Well, you don't want to go just anywhere. Some of these places have pirates or earthquakes or ladyboys. Or all three.

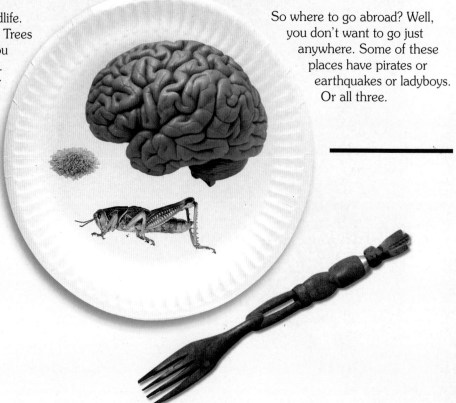

Fig. 1
Typical meal abroad

Source:
Our Trevor

Fig. 2
Abroad = spiders
that can kill you

MAMMY'S LIST OF WHERE IT'S SAFE TO GO

CANADA:
Poor man's America

AMERICA:
SuperIreland

ENGLAND:
Same plugs

FRANCE:
Lourdes only

AFRICA:
To spread the Lord's word only

England – nice and near, and the plugs are the same.

France – but only for Lourdes. Forget the rest. It's one big farm.

America – it's basically SuperIreland. A whole feckin' continent full of family.

Canada – if you can't afford America.

Australia – hot and huge. Just the way I like 'em.

Africa – but only to spread the Lord's word.

China – never been there, but it's where my TV's from, and they do sweet and sour prawn balls. What's not to like?

CHINA:
Sweet and sour prawn balls

AUSTRALIA:
Hot and huge

Anywhere else is unnecessary. Especially if it ends in '-stan'. That's where all the trouble starts. There's never been anywhere nice with a 'stan' in it. Even Hilda O'Loughlin's place was nicer after her Stan walked out. I take that as a powerful sign.

I don't understand why anyone needs to travel anyway. The further you go, the further you have to come back home, unless you're a snail, with your house on your back. When God made them move at a snail's own pace, He did it to prove a point.

ADVERTISING

Feck it, but it's everywhere. You can't take a quiet shit by yourself down Foley's without getting a faceful of some advert on the back of the door where there used to be a perfectly good drawing of a cock and balls and some useful phone numbers.

Advertising is like death. No one wants it, it keeps being shoved in your face, it's never going away, and there's nothing you can do about it except close your eyes and wish the world was different.

I don't need to be told what I want. I know what I want. Because I want it. (Though I suppose without that leaflet that fell out the *Sunday Mail*, I'd never have known I wanted those waterproof gardening slacks that have let Grandad sleep through the night.) And what those buffoons in the stupid glasses get paid for doing it. Jaysus. I've written 50 million words for this book, and I bet I got paid less than they do for coming up with 'Because I'm worth it'. You feckin' aren't.

Any fecker could do it. Here's one for you.

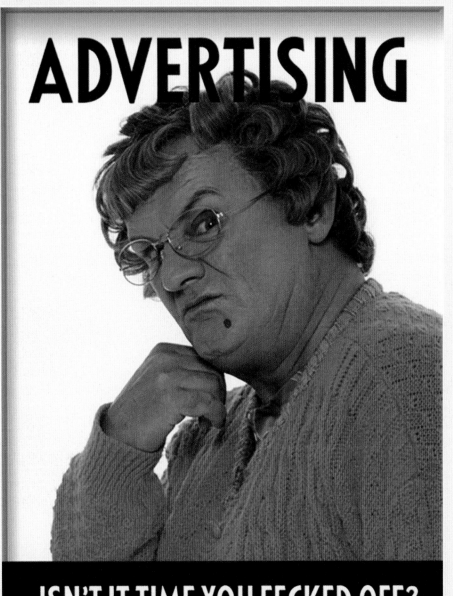

AEROPLANES

A lot of people are frightened of flying. I can't understand that. Flying's fine. It's suddenly stopping feckin' flying that scares the bejaysus out of me.

Ginny Walsh from the Barnardo's shop won't fly until she's had a cracking great fist of drugs. By the time she's got that lot down her neck, I tell you, she doesn't need a feckin' plane.

But, like most things, you can conquer your fear with knowledge, which is sort of what this book's all about. You can turn a terrifying ordeal into a bearable one if you study the theory upfront so you know the ins and outs. That's what I told Maria about her wedding night.

People worry that a plane is too heavy to fly, but that ignores what they call 'the physics', which means it's actually impossible for a plane not to fly. Amazing, isn't it? It's why they have to tempt the planes out of the sky with those little table tennis bats. 'Come down, we'll have ourselves

a nice little game of ping-pong ...' Otherwise the planes'd be up there all the time and none of us could get off for the Duty Free.

So how does a plane stay in the air? Well, I remember Dermot getting me to do some physics homework once, so I know this is good, and it will come as a great comfort to any nervous flyers out there.

How does a plane fly?
Feathers.

Flying things need feathers. Stands to reason. They're lighter than air, so they fly. The only thing that flies without feathers is a bee, and scientists say they've no feckin' idea how that one works. Seen Dumbo? How does the elephant fly? It's got a little feather in its trunk. One tiny feather's all it takes to get a feckin' great elephant up there. So that's science.

Health and safety means they won't rely on just the one feather, though, so every plane is secretly filled with feathers, like a pillow.* It's no problem because feathers are so light they actually make the plane weigh less than it did when it came out of the box. Sure the men who invented planes are embarrassed about it. They're men. They don't want to admit their big flying metal Johnson is all fluffy inside like a baby chick. So you listen to them and it's all about thrust and cockpits. I ask you, is it ever about anything feckin' else? So they hide the feathers inside, everywhere. The whole thing. Stuffed full of feathers. And that's why they give you feck all space for your baggage. Especially Ryanair.

Now you're not so worried about flying, are you? Might sound crazy, but it's a fact. I know it's a fact because Dermot's teacher wrote an 'F' on it. Which is teacher's shorthand for 'fact'.

---

*Although I haven't worked out why pillows don't fly

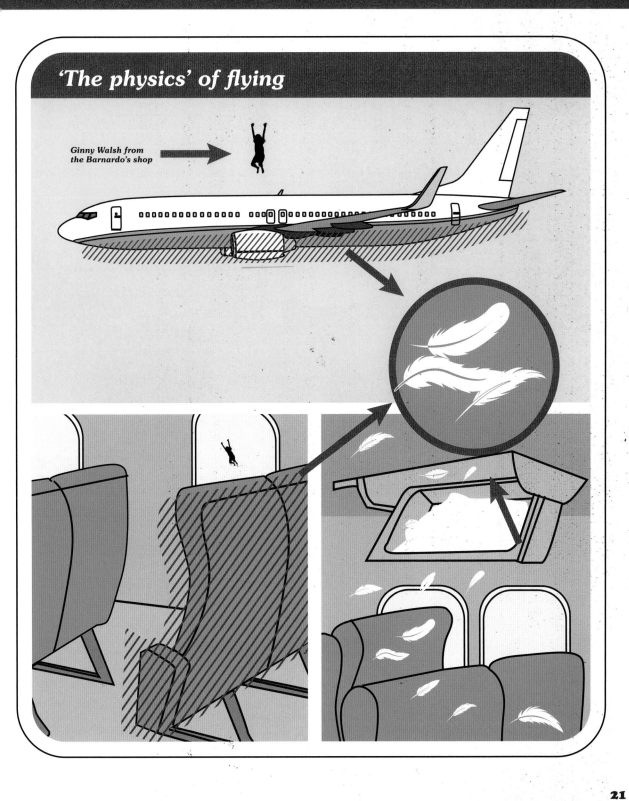

'The physics' of flying

Ginny Walsh from
the Barnardo's shop

AFTERLIFE, THE

If there is some sort of life after death, it's no use to us here and hardly news to anyone on the other side, so forget about it and get on with enjoying the life we definitely know we've got. What do you want two lives for anyway? One for using and one to keep clean for best? Bugger that. Get out there and get some stains on the thing.

AIRPORTS

The place nobody minds a plane coming down. Flying's impossible, so they're meant to bore you until you forget that fact. If you've got some hold luggage, make sure you can recognize it instantly when it comes on to the carousel. When I pack for any of my lot, I always fill the front pocket of their travel bag with something that stinks (gorgonzola, tuna sandwich from early in the holiday), and that way they know it's coming before it's even hit the conveyor. Sometimes I even remember to remind them.

SPOT YOUR BAG ON THE CAROUSEL

Travel bag

+

A tuna sandwich (the older the better)

+

Gorgonzola cheese

ALLERGIES

People these days are allergic to everything.
It's just to get attention.

'Oh, I can't eat fish. I'm special.' You're not special. You're a pain in the feckin' arse.

Winnie's Sharon once told me she was 'wheat intolerant'. You come round my house turning your nose up at a perfectly good sandwich, I'll show you feckin' intolerance. But once the idea's there, it spreads like a disease, it really does. Soon Cathy was worrying she might be 'lactose and gluten intolerant'. I told her that was impossible. I wouldn't feed my family any of that foreign muck.

She said lactoses and glutens were things they hide in bread and milk, and that meant milk and bread were both off the menu from now on. Jaysus, that's a crime, that is. And me with a chest freezer full of the stuff. I didn't grow up in a family that went hungry some days to have all that bread and milk go to waste. What am I

meant to do with it? If I put a load of bread and milk out for the bin men, it'd attract a hedgehog the size of a feckin' bus.

Anyway, Cathy got over it. Unlike the lad at Dermot's sixth birthday party with the peanut allergy. Turns out that one isn't made up. Sure, he calmed down in the ambulance, but if I'd known there was peanut in a peanut butter and jam sandwich, I'd have put a warning on them, on a little sign on a cocktail stick. Skull and crossbones. 'These ones are ham. And these ones are poison.'

I don't understand where this everyone's-got-an-allergy business came from. It used to only be the kids at school with glasses who had allergies, now everybody's after copying them. Feck that. The only thing you're meant to copy off kids with glasses is homework.

ARCHITECTURE

The first shed was probably a little cave at the back of the big cave, where the caveman could hide and pretend to be fixing slow punctures on the caveman bikes and hanging up all his flints in size order, when there was caveman washing-up needing doing.

And from there architecture has come on in leaps and bounds, from corner sheds to flat-roofed garden lean-tos to that terrifying thing they've got at number 48. Jaysus alone knows what he's building in there. It's like a Zeppelin hangar. Poor Mrs Brannigan was saying it casts a shadow over her cucumber frame, and this year's crop wouldn't look out of place dangling off the front of a Siberian nudist.

Other buildings include cathedrals, airports, charity shops and boat sheds.

Fig. 1: Early sheds as depicted in ancient cave paintings

Fig. 2: Airports

Fig. 3: Cathedrals

ART

I don't know much about art, but I know what I like. CAKE.

I love cake. I've eaten cakes you wouldn't believe. Cakes that were works of feckin' art. Marie McCrann from Dullea's cake shop can do a Kermit the Frog that looks like it's right off the telly. She did a wedding cake once that had so many tiers it needed planning permission. And until that Tracey Emin makes me a cake, I'm not giving her an inch of respect. Not that I'd eat it. I've seen her bed, so I can only imagine the state of her feckin' kitchen.

There are two sorts of art:

1. Proper Art
2. The sort of silly bollix a five-year-old could knock out

Proper Art would normally have been invented by one of your famous Italian lads, Michael or Angelo, or the Irish one, Leonard O'Davinci, and most of it happened a long time ago. It's fierce hard and you have to be able to do fingers and make stuff smaller in the background, so you don't get it so much now.

There are only two sorts of Proper Art:

1. Paintings of boats and houses
2. Pencil drawings of your kids

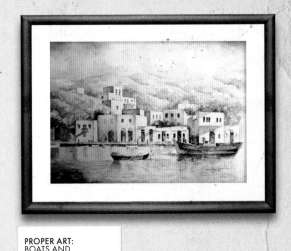

PROPER ART:
BOATS AND
HOUSES

PROPER ART:
PENCIL DRAWINGS
OF YOUR KIDS

BOLLIX ART

ART CONTINUED

Those are both Proper Art, because they look like the thing they're meant to be, and for feck's sake, how much is that to ask? I don't know how anyone could actually forget how many feckin' eyes a woman has, but your art-college lads only went and did. It was probably the paint fumes. (Redser was doing under the stairs with some old paint once and when I looked in on him a couple of hours later, he was sitting there staring pink-eyed at the little disc going round in the electricity meter. 'I thought this jukebox was broken, Agnes,' he said, 'but it sounds all right to me.')

And as for all the splatter pictures and the ones which are just big purple rectangles – what kind of fool calls that art? It's a short step from saying, 'Look, I've done a rectangle all purple, that'll be millions of dollars' to 'Sure, Mrs Brown, I've painted your kitchen wall, that'll be far too much money.' You can see where they get their ideas from.

I think artists forgot how to paint properly some time in the 60s, and I'll go no further than to say they weren't exactly smoking Carroll's Number 1s. Oh, it does even worse things to the brain than paint fumes. Dermot's mate Niall hasn't put shoes on since 2011, and they won't let him back at the Toyota garage. Waste of a fine mind, that was.

Here is a selection of the best art there is – and I know that because Winnie got these on a set of coasters from the Age Action, and they wouldn't put any old shite on coasters – along with some notes on how to understand it, because apparently that's normal.

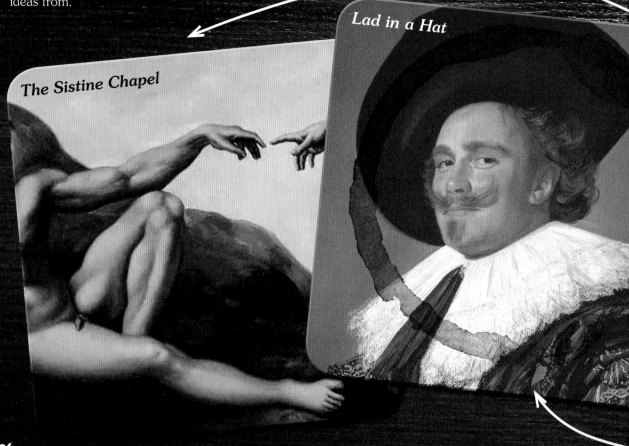

The Sistine Chapel

Lad in a Hat

26

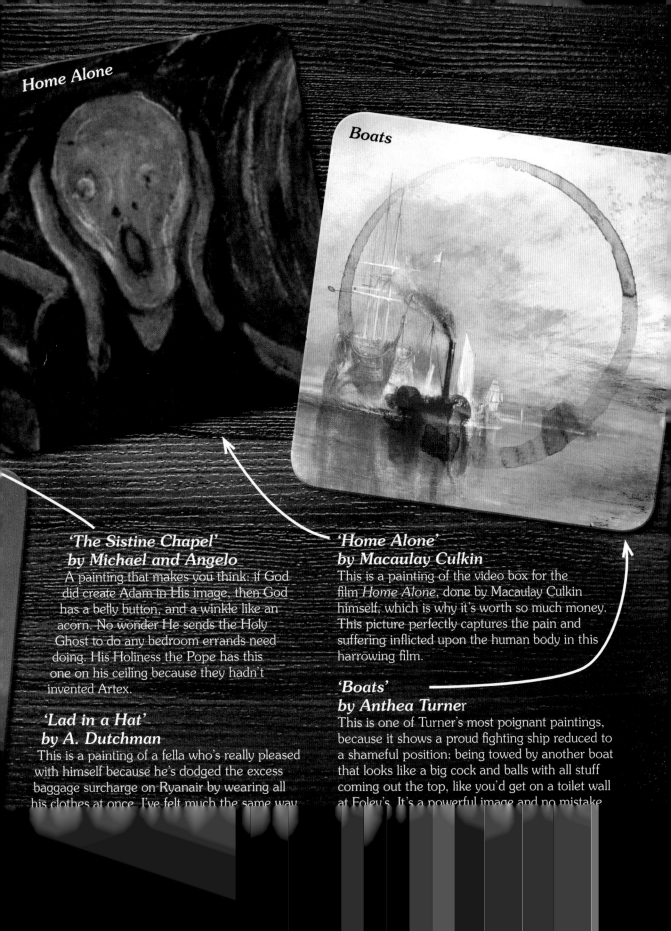

Home Alone

Boats

'The Sistine Chapel'
by Michael and Angelo
A painting that makes you think: if God did create Adam in His image, then God has a belly button, and a winkle like an acorn. No wonder He sends the Holy Ghost to do any bedroom errands need doing. His Holiness the Pope has this one on his ceiling because they hadn't invented Artex.

'Lad in a Hat'
by A. Dutchman
This is a painting of a fella who's really pleased with himself because he's dodged the excess baggage surcharge on Ryanair by wearing all his clothes at once. I've felt much the same way

'Home Alone'
by Macaulay Culkin
This is a painting of the video box for the film *Home Alone*, done by Macaulay Culkin himself, which is why it's worth so much money. This picture perfectly captures the pain and suffering inflicted upon the human body in this harrowing film.

'Boats'
by Anthea Turner
This is one of Turner's most poignant paintings, because it shows a proud fighting ship reduced to a shameful position: being towed by another boat that looks like a big cock and balls with all stuff coming out the top, like you'd get on a toilet wall at Foley's. It's a powerful image and no mistake.

IS FOR...
BALLOONS
BATHS
BEDTIME STORIES
BERMUDA TRIANGLE, THE
BIRDS
BIRTHDAYS
BISCUITS
BLOODY CYCLISTS
BONDAGE
BRAIN, THE
BREAD
BUDGIES
BUSES

BALLOONS

Balloons are a great way to teach the chisellers about the briefness of life without having to flush a hamster down the U-bend. For a harder sense of loss, maybe for an older child, try bursting a balloon animal.

BATHS

You can't beat a bath. We take them for granted now, but when I was a nipper, there was one bath a week, in a tin tub in the kitchen. Every one of us queued up, got in, got scrubbed with a shoe brush, got out, and got rubbed down with a towel. If you were first, you got rubbed down by a dry towel. If you were last, the towel made you even wetter than when you were in the tub. It was like dipping sheep.

The perfect bath needs time. You don't want some fecker interrupting you, needing to do a number two. Even if you close your eyes, the splashing's a terrible distraction.

So before you run a bath, make sure everyone in the family has emptied themselves, or is about to go out somewhere that's got a toilet. Preferably taking Grandad with them, because his insides are a law unto themselves. Now you're ready.

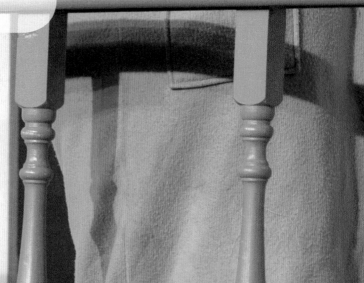

Bubbles. You need bubbles. Otherwise you've got nothing nice to look at and you'll end up staring at your body wobbling to and fro, and pulling the grey hairs out of your bits one by one, which is a fine way to spoil a bath. (If not for you, for the next person who uses the water.)

You can take a book in, but it will curl. But some people quite like that. Mark tells me Betty always takes in a little pile of books off the classy end of the shelf – you know, ones she's been bought that she's never got round to reading. I don't reckon she reads a word of them, but once they've fattened up a bit, they take up more space on the shelf, and with the spines all broken with damp, that's got to impress visitors.

I prefer the radio. Stick on something nice – something with tunes you can sing, or someone with a lovely seductive voice to spend some time with, alone, if you get my drift. No sport, though. If you start cheering and swearing, your blood pressure will go sky-high, what with the hot bath, and you might pass out.

And that's the other thing: make it as hot as you can fuckin' bear. It should take you about twenty minutes just to get into the thing. Get in bit by bit. Start with just one foot. You can tell when you're ready for the next bit because you've stopped crying.

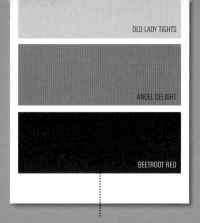

OLD LADY TIGHTS

ANGEL DELIGHT

BEETROOT RED

Once you're in, you should go the colour of a beetroot. If you don't, add some more hot water.

Anything less than half an hour in the bath is technically a shower. So take your time. If you haven't got a clock in there, you can tell how long you've been in by your wrinkling. If your fingertips don't look like an old fella's ballbag, you haven't been in there long enough. (Sure, what happens to old fellas' ballbags in the bath? Do they go the opposite way, and look all smooth and young? If you know this, write to me at the usual address. Include a photo if you can.)

33

BEDTIME STORIES

Even if it's the only book to hand, try to avoid any bedtime story where a brain-damaged nightwatchman is burned to death in an abattoir fire and returns from the grave to rip sleeping kiddies' arms off with a pair of garden shears.

Or a picture book with a sixteen-page tongue twister about a beetle that drives you feckin' postal when they ask for it night after feckin' night. Screaming is very stressful at bedtime, whether it's them doing it or you. You're meant to be sending them to sleep, remember. I recommend the telephone directory. It's surprisingly soothing, and if you do the voices, they barely notice.

The only triangular body of water on the planet

Caribbean Sea

BERMUDA TRIANGLE, THE

The Bermuda Triangle is the only triangular body of water on the planet, other than the gap down the side of the fridge where the sink leaks. Stuff goes in the Bermuda Triangle and just vanishes. Like the penny jar on top of the boiler. That's a mystery they need to get someone in to look at. Thirty years I've been putting change in there, and it's never got full. Ever since Dermot got tall enough to reach it. Feckin' miracle that is.

BIRDS

Animals who've moved into God's loft conversion. In winter, the birds in your garden need you.

Two facts I never tire of telling people:

*A pair of dangling fat balls can fill any nearby bush with thrush...
And tits like coconuts.*

BIRTHDAYS

I've not had a birthday in years.

Kicking the habit was hard, but I found there were other ways to get cards and cake (overdue library books, wakes) and before long I didn't even miss them. I've been happily free of the craving now since my late 30s, back in March. I'm a convert. They're a filthy addiction and I'm better now I'm clean.

BISCUITS

I always say there is nothing, nothing, better than a nice cup of tea. Except for one other thing, and that's a nice cup of tea and a biscuit. Which are actually two things, so I stand by my original statement. Don't try and catch me out. I'm sharp as pie, me.

The most important thing is to choose the right biscuit. If it's too fancy, you can get distracted, ruining a perfectly good cup of tea. There's nothing worse than a biscuit with airs, or what I like to call an 'air biscuit'. Quite spoils the atmosphere.

Too plain and you might as well eat the coaster. I've heard tell that some people eat biscuits without a cup of tea at all, but then I've heard that some people eat Sunday dinner without ketchup, and I'm not sure I believe that either.

I say you can tell a lot about someone by what biscuit they like. I call it my Biscuit Zodiac. It's the key to unlocking the mysteries of personality. Simply look at what someone's plopped in their saucer, and you can decode their whole character. I know! It's spooky!

This idea is copyright Agnes Brown, by the way, as usual. Usual address. No circulars…

THE BISCUIT ZODIAC

& CUSTARDUS
The Custard Cream

If you're a Custard Cream person, you are very busy on the surface with all swirly lines that look like a posh gate, but if anyone takes the trouble to look inside, they'll find your heart is soft, sweet and a bit like one of those foam pads they use to stop furniture marking wood floors, but sort of hearing-aid colour.

@ HOBNOBUS
The Hobnob

When the going gets hot, Hobnob people are notoriously flaky, often going to pieces and crumbling, leaving this horrible gritty muck at the bottom of the cup. Hobnobuses also have a notoriously dry character and can give you a fearsome cough.

⊘ DIGESTO
The Digestive

Boring and brown, a real all-rounder, Digestive people are just, you know, there. They'll do if there's nobody better nearby, but are surprisingly good with cheese triangles.

5/8 BOURBONIUS
The Bourbon

Though dark and mysterious, a Bourbon person is a straight-up-and-down standby you can rely on not to crack or drop you in the drink. If you are a Bourbon person, do watch out for people trying to take your top off to get to your good bits.

€ WAFER
The Pink Wafer

As a Pink Wafer person, you're colourful and exciting at first, but a terrible letdown when you get dipped in tea, which makes you sad and floppy like a wet cardboard box flattened under a skip. Sure, you're fun at a party, and you're good with children, but you're not someone anybody asks to tea unless they don't know any Fruit Shortcakes.

§ GARIBALDUS
The Garibaldi

One of the 'earth signs' of the Biscuit Zodiac, a Garibaldi person is outgoing but grounded, with a love of art, food and the finer things. They are also rectangular and full of squashed flies.

£ CHOCO
The Choco Liebniz

The Choco Liebniz person thinks they're the bee's feckin' pyjamas, with their fancy foreign continental ways, turning up at your house, acting like they're better than you because they're half-covered in chocolate. But underneath all that, they're just a square Rich Tea with ideas above its feckin' station, and don't I know it, Hilliary feckin' Nicolson, bringing me biscuits in a feckin' cardboard box, as if cellophane's not good enough for you. And even though I thought about it, I didn't throw the rest of the packet in the bin after you'd gone, because I'm better than that. I gave them to the dog. And he was sick. Because you shouldn't give dogs chocolate. I hope you're happy now.

¶ TUNNOX
The Teacake

Teacake people have big, round, brown chocolate heads and squashy marshmallow bottoms. They come in a pack of six and are wrapped in tinfoil. I really shouldn't have eaten all of them; I was saving them for Sunday tea. Tunnox is a sign strongly associated with regret.

JAFFUS
The Jaffa Cake

The Jaffa Cake person is slightly smaller than you remember, but deep down surprisingly fruity and covered in chocolate. Jaffas melt easily and can leave stubborn brown stains on pale clothes (see Laundry). If you leave them alone too long, their bottoms go hard. I'll be honest, this is more true of the biscuit than the person, but my point stands.

¥ JAMMINI
The Jammie Dodger

A Jammie Dodger person is attractive and reliable, with a heart of purest jam.

% CRUNCHIBUS
The Fruit Shortcake

Fruit Shortcake people are hard and sweet but with a wobbly edge, and once you've met one, you'll want to eat the whole packet. Do I mean that? No. This isn't working quite as well as I'd hoped. I'm trying to make this about personality types, but now I keep thinking about biscuits and forgetting it's meant to be about people too. Maybe if I have a biscuit, I'll stop thinking about biscuits. That's it. Hold on there. I'll be right back.

ⓘ WEASLIUS
The Ginger Nut

One of the 'fire signs' of the Biscuit Zodiac, Ginger Nut people are rock hard. They wouldn't melt if you dipped them in a feckin' volcano (see Volcanoes), which you might think was good but it's actually a pain in the arse if you're hoping to eat more than three of these in a row without booking a visit to the dentist. Winnie eats these for her digestion, but she'd be better off chewing on a manhole cover. Feck. Wouldn't you know it, I'm just talking about biscuits again. People. People. Ginger Nut people are animal lovers who trust easily and enjoy new challenges. You will meet a tall dark biscuit. Stranger! Tall dark stranger.

BLOODY CYCLISTS

To my mind, a cyclist is a nice silver-haired man or woman sitting upright on a bike with mudguards and a basket on the front. They might even have a little hat. They'll pull up, wave you across their path and say, 'Good morning.' If you're in their way, they'll probably ring a bell that sounds like a fairy having a cough. Lovely.

That's a cyclist. But this isn't about cyclists. It's about Bloody Cyclists.

A Bloody Cyclist doesn't look like a human being. A Bloody Cyclist looks like a giant feckin' cockroach with shiny legs and a shiny head, head to toe in that feckin' awful new yellow they came up with a few years ago. The one that's the colour of a sinus headache.

You can't see their eyes, because they've got weird moustache-shaped sunglasses on. You can't see their hair, because they're wearing a helmet made from a spaceship nosecone. What you can see is every feckin' ripple in their flesh, because they're wearing a top and trousers that might as well have been painted on by an art student pervert.

And they're bent forward, rocketing along like the paramilitary wing of the Tour de Feckin' France, a 50-mile-an-hour fundamentalist with a fatwa against pedestrians.

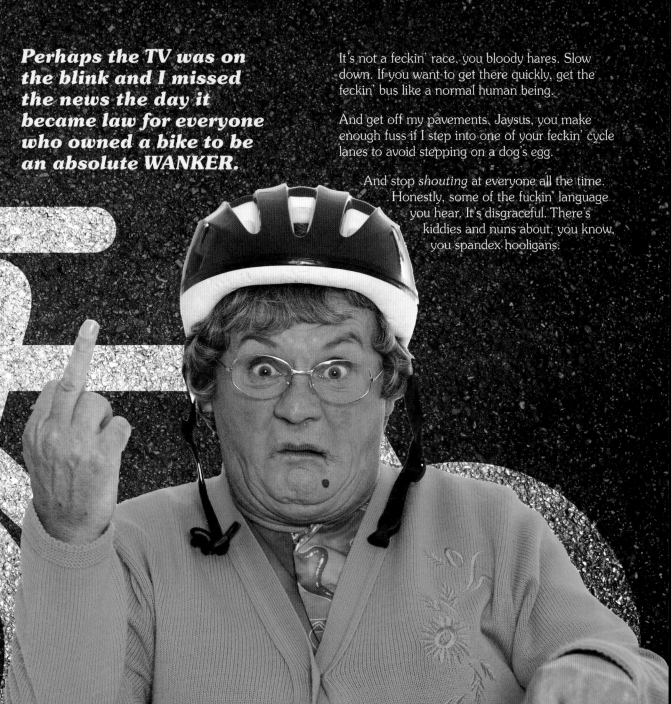

Perhaps the TV was on the blink and I missed the news the day it became law for everyone who owned a bike to be an absolute WANKER.

It's not a feckin' race, you bloody hares. Slow down. If you want to get there quickly, get the feckin' bus like a normal human being.

And get off my pavements. Jaysus, you make enough fuss if I step into one of your feckin' cycle lanes to avoid stepping on a dog's egg.

And stop *shouting* at everyone all the time. Honestly, some of the fuckin' language you hear. It's disgraceful. There's kiddies and nuns about, you know, you spandex hooligans.

43

BONDAGE

People get up to all sorts in the privacy of their own homes. You wouldn't believe. Some of the mousiest-looking people. Winnie swears blind the man with the combover and the bottle-bottom specs who photocopies her wordsearches down the library is pierced like a key ring downstairs. She says she saw him get stuck fast by the groin to the magnetic plate they use to check the books out, though it might have been the button fly on his trousers. Anyway, the world's full of surprises.

Bondage is spicing up bedroom you-know-what by hurting yourself. To be honest, you get to a certain age and any sexy shenanigans beyond having a quiet moment thinking about Daniel O'Donnell is effectively bondage, just because your back isn't up to it. It's still ninety seconds of moaning and groaning in the dark, but for different reasons.

'Just thinking about Daniel O'Donnell is effectively bondage'

Winnie insists that everyone's into tying themselves up and clamping themselves and that. She said that she and Jacko tried it a few times during hospital visiting hours. They drew the curtains and did something I'm not sure I even understand using the traction brace. Her tip: don't use the drip to tie your wrists because it sets the alarm off and the nurse comes. This book is nothing if it's not the voice of experience.

I wouldn't advise it myself. I tried that auto-aspidistrazation once and I couldn't get Redser out of the bin bag afterwards. It was one of those reinforced garden sacks and I was five minutes hacking at it with the sharp end of a key. It's hardly *Fifty Shades of Grey*. More like *Fifty Sheds*.

Winnie's Sharon held one of those Ann Stunners parties. She told me she bought a pair of fluffy handcuffs and a rabbit. Now, I can see the appeal of a rabbit – lovely animal to have around the house. (Except you can't tell rabbit food from rabbit poo. And if you can't, who says the rabbit can?) But here's the funny thing: Sharon said it like it was a secret. Why you'd want to keep a bunny secret is beyond me. But fluffy handcuffs? You've lost me there, love. They might look nice on, but what happens when you want to use a knife and fork or spread your arms? And what's any of this to do with the bedroom? If you ask me, that Ann Stunners must have seen her coming a mile off.

BRAIN, THE

There are two parts of a brain: the woman's brain, which is the whole brain, and the man's brain, which is the half a man uses for remembering where spanners are and who was in goal for things.

Brains look a lot like cauliflowers, which makes you think. What if cauliflowers got only a slight little bit more intelligent and started to think for themselves? Maybe they don't like all that cheese. Maybe they're angry about the Things We Do to them. That'd be some scary film there. (Idea copyright Agnes Brown, usual address.)

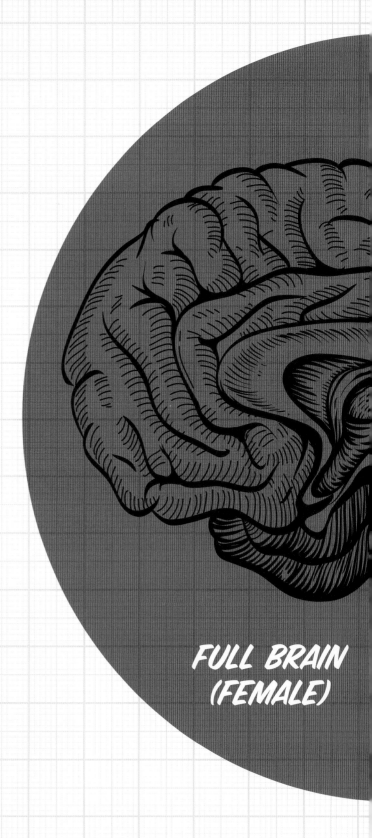

FULL BRAIN
(FEMALE)

HALF BRAIN (MALE)

BREAD

The Bible says: 'Man cannot live on bread alone.' But after Pauline Langer fell under that tram, her man Cobbo lived on nothing but toast for months, and he was completely alone, so that shows you that the Bible sometimes gets stuff wrong, and not just in the bit with Noah's Ark and the Flood, where God seems perfectly happy about not punishing any of the birds or the fish for their sins, when you can bet your last brass farthing they were up to just as much filth as the hedgehogs.

Bread comes in two types:

1. White bread
2. Brown bread

Brown bread is also known as 'toast'. I couldn't believe it, all those years ago, when they started selling it in packets. A whole loaf of ready-browned bread. I ask you. How bone feckin' idle can you be? It's like ready-grated cheese or those pizzas they make for kids with all the pineapple already picked off.

A few years ago I noticed Dermot's hair had started to fall out, and we realized he'd eaten nothing but cheese on toast for weeks. He was really busy, and some of those court hearings start very early, so he wasn't looking after himself. I took him in hand, like any Mammy would when she sees her own child in danger. I said, 'You've got to look after yourself. You can't just eat cheese on toast,' and forced some pizza down him sharpish, plus a side order of garlic bread. Rory said he needed vegetables, but I've just checked on Cathy's eyepad thing, and most of the internet reckons garlic's a vegetable, except some lad in Ohio who says it's a fish. Still, that'd mean it was full of the Omega whatnot, and Dermot's not dead, so who's the expert now?

It's not just food, either. Here are some of the handy things I've used toast for.

Fancy-Dress Costume

One time Mark's halfway out the door ready for school when he tells me it's charity fancy-dress day. I had no time at all, but a Mammy is used to thinking on her feet. And using only a few economy loaves and some string, I had him the most amazing superhero costume. I'll admit, some of the kids in his class wouldn't believe there was a Toastman, but by then most of the costume had fallen off, and he could say he'd come as Toastman's secret alter ego, Mark Kent. By the way, if anyone from a big Hollywood studio is reading this and wants to make a series of Toastman films, this is copyright me, and you're not having it without talking to me directly (business class flights only, unlimited Duty Free).

Scourer

A slice of burned toast dipped in Fairy gets pans up nice and black, and when it gets soggy, just toast some more. Also works a treat in the bath on dead skin.

Fort

Another great thing for the kiddies. When they want to play in a fort, don't take the cushions off the sofa, just toast up a few slices and lean them against each other in the front room. It's quite small, but it'll fit an Action Man or the hamster, until Grandad gets peckish.

Devotional Picture

From what I read in the magazines, Jesus is always after magically making his face appear on slices of toast. (Maybe that's what they did before photographs were invented.) So, if you're expecting a visit from a priest and you want to God Up your house a bit before he arrives, pop the toaster on, say a quick prayer and cross your fingers.

Frisbee

I haven't tried this one, but many's the afternoon I've whiled away trying to land a slice directly in Grandad's snoring gob from the other side of the room, so I've no reason to think it wouldn't work in the park.

Birthday Card

How many times have you checked the calendar and noticed it's someone's birthday tomorrow and you've forgotten to send a card? Well, the mail has to take anything with a stamp on it, so if you toast some bread good and black, you can scrape a greeting and the address out of the charcoal, and pop a stamp on. Bingo! A novelty birthday postcard. Or 'toastcard', if you like. And if you're really lucky, you might get a nice holy image of Jesus on the 'picture' side.

BUDGIES

There's nothing nicer than having a pet. Except a pint of cider. Or a plate of sausages. Or a bit of a grown-up cuddle. Or even a nice weekend at the coast. Come to think of it, there's lots of nicer things than having a pet (see Pet Care).

I'll start again.

Having a pet can be lovely and rewarding. Seeing the look on a dog's face when you give it the leftovers from a Sunday roast, its tongue all lolling and dripping, is like seeing a nipper at Christmas. A big hairy stupid nipper, to be fair, that's not got the hang of the potty yet and has picked up a bit of a residual stink, but it's lovely anyway.

But a dog needs walking. And if your hips these days are less an unstoppable dance engine and more a pair of stone mill wheels that long since stopped doing anything useful, you might struggle with all the exercise. (Of course, there's getting your Alsatian to pull you round in your late husband's sidecar, like Mad Mammy Cunningham did until the dog chased a rat into a culvert. Good job that sidecar floated and she had her hipflask.)

**And some pets are just
plain pointless.**

Stick insects:
about as exciting as keeping pet pencils

Rabbits:
like locking soft toys in prison

Fish:
like watching a foreign kiddies'
programme with the sound down

Cats: bastards (see above)

**So if you need a pet that's fun,
friendly and feck-all effort, you
want a budgie.**

My Mammy always had budgies. There was Buster,
Chaplin, Greta, Groucho, Tallulah and Keith
(no, me neither). None of them lasted long, what
with my Mammy's eyesight and her vicious hoover.
But they were all lovely little things, especially
Tallulah, who could say 'Knackers to yous all'
crystal clear.

And I kept budgies for many years. Some of them were
luckier than others. Sausages I unfortunately flew into
the Xpelair. Sausages II was luckier, until Grandad sat
on her. Bob Dylan was got by the hoover but survived,
only to fall off his little perch and die of shock a few days
later. I think the dust did it for him. Wendy was a terrible
bugger. Always shitting everywhere (see Laundry).
We had to feed her scrambled egg to keep her shut.
And that didn't feel right. A bird, eating scrambled egg?
Doesn't bear thinking about.

Everyone's favourite was Peccadildo. (Winnie named him.) He was a lovely little bird. Bright blue, handsome as hell, and he knew it. Strutted up and down his perch, admiring himself in the mirror. Very much the Robert Redford of the budgerigar world. What a fella.

I taught him to say 'Who are you looking at?' Cathy taught him to say 'Pretty boy'. And someone – I can't be sure who – taught him to say 'Shut up, you damn bird'. Plus he did a terrific impression of Redser burping. He was such an entertaining lad. Then one day the vet had to look at him, and said, 'Agnes, how long have you had her?' Turns out he wasn't a fella after all. He was a little loudmouthed cow who liked looking at herself in the mirror and flirting with everyone. Basically a flying floozy.

Still, budgies are a piece of piss to keep. All's you need are:

- a cage
- plenty of sandpaper
- a bell and a mirror to keep the little bugger entertained
- shares in Trill
- good sturdy shoes to kick next-door's cat out when it comes sniffing
- a TV loud enough to get over its fierce chirping when it hears the birds outside

And – though I learned this a bit late in the day – the way you tell whether they're a lad or a lass is by the colour of their nostrils. Boys are blue, girls are pink. If you can't remember that, you're too far gone to start thinking about owning budgies now. Trim the top off a feather duster and Sellotape it to the perch, it'll be safer.

Shut up, you damn bird! Shut up, you damn bird! Shut up, you damn bird!

Left:
Peccadildo

Right:
Robert Redford

BUSES

The amount of traffic in town sometimes, there's almost no point in getting a bus.

I've hopped on one to save the walk on a hot summer's day and ended up locked in this feckin' greenhouse on wheels, face pressed against the glass, shopping melting on my lap, the engine puttering up my arse, stiller than a snail that's hitched a lift on the back of a dead tortoise. Jaysus. I'd have got home quicker if I'd jumped into a branch of WHSmiths.

Greenhouse on bucking wheels!

~~Bus~~ Stop

69° NEXT STOP

FECKIN' SHIT

is for...

CARAVANS

Livin' La Vida Leprechaun. A caravan is the perfect way to go on holiday if you are 3'6" tall or less, otherwise it's like being a giant trapped in a doll's house. Nobody's arse is that small, nobody eats miniature food, nobody can wash in a sink that size, and there aren't enough plasters in the tiny first aid box for all the times you smash your head on a low something or other. And there's not enough room for all the furniture you need, so the thing you sleep on doubles as a sofa, and a table and a window. It would be more comfortable to spend a week in a feckin' shoe. I won't go on holiday now unless I'm guaranteed a proper room, slot machines in the bar and a Sunday evening cabaret with at least one surviving Dooley.

CAR REPAIRS

I never learned to drive, and I certainly never learned to fix a car. You know what they say: you don't marry a dog and bark yourself. But Redser always bought his cars from friends of men down the pub, so even as a passenger, I've seen precious little driving and a feckload of emergency repairs, so I probably know more about cars than that Jeremy Paxman off Top Gear.

Jaysus, some of our cars were sights to behold: write-offs, lemons, cut-and-shuts. The first time I'd ever been in a car with the front and the back end the same feckin' colour was in the ambulance after we were overcome by smoke on the ring road outside Lusk.

There are two places to fix a car:

1. In the garage
2. By the side of the road

The garage is better. It's peaceful and cool, and men are nearly as happy in there as they are in the toilet.

TO AGNES,

WITH ALL MY LOVE, REDSER.
IF YOU DON'T WANT THESE,
I'LL TAKE THEM!

Some of the tenderest moments of my marriage were spent placing a cup of tea next to a pair of feet sticking out from under a bollixed car. You can not say a word, or talk for hours, whatever you fancy. They won't know. They can nod off under there, and as long as there's a load of bolts on a filthy towel nearby, you're none the wiser. It's a little eye of calm in the middle of the marital storm.

Ginny O'Hanrahan claims she's only ever exchanged two words with her Ally in the whole of her marriage ('I do') that weren't directed at a pair of garage slippers, and the pair of them have been happily together for forty-six years this April. (The O'Hanrahans, not the slippers.)

Car repairs by the side of the road are a different kettle of shit. Sweet Mary, a hot car full of kids, a steaming radiator and an open bonnet can put your marriage under more strain than a weightlifter's jockstrap. If the AA did roadside divorces, they'd clean up.

So it pays to be prepared and know what to expect, even as a passenger. You don't need to be a technical genius, just know how to spot a few tell-tale signs and what to do.

OCTOBER

1	2	3	4	5	6	7
8	9	10	11	12	13	14
15	16	17	18	19	20	21
22	23	24	25	26	27	28
29	30	31				

SHIT FIT

Symptom:

Regular tapping noise from engine.

Course of Action:

Pull in at side of road immediately. Man should stand in pissing rain for an hour staring at the engine, insisting he doesn't need to call a feckin' man in a van for a tapping noise, it'll be one of these needs tightening, while the kids should hit each other in the back and you try to eke a family bag of Tayto Cheese and Onion out between them and pretend that's lunch.

Symptom:

Brake pedal vibrates when depressed.

Course of Action:

Pull in at side of road immediately. Man should walk two to three miles in hail that could strip the paint off a lighthouse to find working roadside phone while you try to stop the kids climbing into the front where they've worked out they can dodge the child locks and have a race across the dual carriageway.

Symptom:

Crack in windscreen.

Course of Action:

If the crack is less than an inch, don't panic: the man should continue driving and you should get it repaired at a later date. If the crack is longer than an inch, the man should continue driving while you point out every couple of minutes that you're pretty sure it's getting bigger, describing in detail how awful it would be if the whole feckin' thing blew in and went all over the children, and how are they ever going to find love with a face like a scored ham?

Symptom:

Smoke from exhaust while idling in traffic.

Course of Action:

Man should insist it's probably fine. You should suggest a game of I Spy to keep the kids amused and repeatedly choose 'S for smoke' until he pulls over and calls the feckin' AA like a responsible feckin' adult.

Symptom:

Engine doesn't turn over.

Course of Action:

Man should try the key in the ignition and say, 'Come on,' gently, while it doesn't start. Then again, slightly louder, while it doesn't start. Then keep repeating, louder and louder, and with bluer and bluer language, while it doesn't start. Ideally he should call it every name under the feckin' sun while it doesn't start. Eventually, man will find a friend who'll push it and it'll sort of cough into life. This is all best observed from the front-room window.

CHILDREN'S TELEVISION

Jaysus, what's that all about now? I don't really get how Dermot and Maria's remote control works since they paid for that premium service where they can steal next-door's telly, but I was sitting the triplets once and I found this noisy show about adding up, with numbers and bright colours and all these characters with weird names like Nasdack and Footsie, and I couldn't understand a feckin' word. But the babbies seemed to like it. They went off to sleep a bit after I did.

CHIPS

Chips are the other foundation of a healthy diet next to sausages, which is where you'll usually find them. I think of them as little sausages made of potato. Potatoes are, of course, a vegetable, but if you turn them into chips, they're quite nice regardless.

OVEN CHIPS

One of the few foods to come with the cooking instructions in its name. Marketed to the sort of people who might otherwise put them in the washing machine or the boot of the car.

FRENCH FRIES

'French Fried Potatoes' are an American idea but they blame the French, and I can see why. No feckin' use. Like eating a fistful of hot string. Barely big enough to hit with a shake of salt. Served with burgers and hot dogs and that. Can you imagine having a nice bit of battered fish and a mess of piddly French fries? No. Because they're not *chips*.

SAUTÉ POTATOES

What the French call fried potatoes, to tell them apart from French Fried Potatoes. (No. Me neither.) The same thing, but round rather than long. It's like someone cut a carrot into coins rather than sticks and tried to pass it off as a different vegetable. These aren't chips, they're damp crisps. Shameless.

CRINKLE-CUT CHIPS

You don't see these too much any more. They were all the go in the 70s, like flared carrots and balaclavas, and the kids loved them for some reason. I suppose because they looked like building blocks. My Rory, bless him, wouldn't touch straight chips with a bargepole. I suppose the signs were all there.

CRISPS

The most expensive way of selling a potato that mankind has ever thought up. Next time you pick up a bag of Tayto from the paper shop, pour out the crisps from your bag onto the counter and build them back into as much of a potato as you can manage. Deduct a couple of pennies for fat and ask for your money back to cover the difference.

MAMMY CHIPS

The Mammy Chip is the queen of chips. Thicker than your finger, you get a maximum of three chips per potato, each hotter than the sun. I'm not spending all day cutting your feckin' chips up, there's laundry needs doing (see Laundry).

MAMMY'S CHIP RECIPE

Peel your taters. Cut each one into chunks (two for a golf-ball sized spud, three for one the size of a grapefruit). Make plenty of them. Pop them in the chip pan with enough oil to cover them, and put on a lid, for safety. Turn the heat up to full whack. Go to the pub and have one (1) pint of cider. When you get home, you should have a pan of delicious chips and a load of firemen to share it with. Make sure you put on enough for the boys in red. It's fierce hungry work putting out a chip-pan fire.

Holy Smokes

Smoking kills kittens

CIGARETTES

Cigarettes are God's way of telling you to give up smoking. Unfortunately, they're also God's way of telling you to take up smoking in the first place.

That's the thing, you see: He moves in mysterious ways.

And what He gives with one hand, He takes away with another. So when God offers you a cigarette, He's going to snatch it off you pretty sharpish. That's why smokers always look so panicked.

CLASSICAL MUSIC

Classical Music is anything with violins in, like The Dubliners, the Harry Potter films and some of the posher songs by Daniel O'Donnell.

The concerts are very refined affairs. You're not allowed to throw your underwear, in case it gets tangled in a harp. The band gets dressed up like The Temptations, so you're expected to put on your best frock. All the songs have numbers and letters instead of names, like a move in Battleships, so you don't know what they're about. And most of them haven't got words either. I went for the fireworks, but I slept through most of it and only woke up in time for the one from the bread advert. Composers of Classical Music who I may have heard of include Wolfgang, Amadeus, Mozart, Ludwig Van Potato Van, Handle and Gary Barlow.

COATS

Coats are a form of clothing which was invented in Ancient Times by the Ancient Persians (who also invented those hairba cats cough up). The coat was a primitive way of keeping out the cold because nobody had yet invented the cardigan.

Unlike the modern cardigan, which can be worn both indoors and outdoors, the coat is fo outdoors only. This means you have to decide when to take the thing off, a problem nobody has with a cardigan, which is worn all the time and unbuttoned only for moving heavy furnitu and unavoidable marital business between the months of June and August.

All the taking on and off with coats is what causes so many problems with The Benefit.

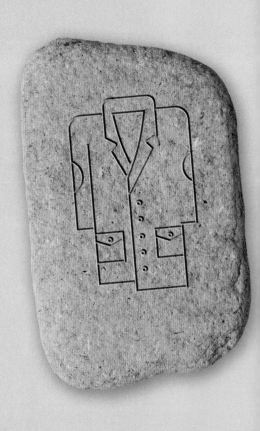

THE BENEFIT

Nobody really knows what The Benefit is, and there's no scientific unit for measuring it like there is for electricity or shoe size, but every Mammy understands The Benefit and how important it is that their children feel it, and that this is dangerously at risk if they wear a coat indoors for any more than the minimal time required to get it to a peg or the back of a kitchen chair.

I've done a formula for The Benefit. Yes I have. No, you feck off.

$$B = \frac{CH}{CT}$$

B is 'The Benefit' in this formula, if we assume that CH is the central heating setting, assume CT is the length of time the coat has been on, and assume that I've no idea what one of these formula things is but have seen them on blackboards behind Brains on *Thunderbirds*, and I remember they sort of look like that. Maybe I should put an 'x' in there.

$$B = \frac{CH}{CTx}$$

Much better. The little 'x' means 'love Mammy', and that's what The Benefit's all about. Love. I'm OK in my cardigan, but I'm not having a child of mine found frozen to death on the doorstep because they kept their parka done up in a kitchen full of spud steam.

Coats are also good ways of keeping a pair of mittens from going missing, using a length of elastic threaded through the arms. Dermot won't thank me for blabbing this, but until he was 23, I was doing the same with his socks. One time he forgot, pulled his shoes off in a hurry and kneed himself in the eye.

CREOSOTE

Science will one day be able to explain creosote. It's not a paint or a varnish or an oil, it's a thing all of its own. And it's a drug, too. It must be, because it's got an amazing medical property: it can make men happy.

Redser was forever creosoting our fence. He was like your man who paints the Forth Bridge – finishes the job, just has time for a cup of tea and a couple of interviews with the local TV, and then has to start all over again.

Looking back, I suppose Redser might have been addicted to creosote. But, for God's sake, if it made him happy and it wasn't doing him any harm, so what?

If you want a happy hubby, find him something to creosote. The side gate, the dog kennel, the crucifix outside St Banban's, Hobbler Reardon's leg. Anything'll do. Only don't let him use it on his hair when he starts going grey. It's a bastard to get out of bath towels.

IS FOR...

DALLAS
DENTISTS
DINOSAURS
DREAMS

DERMOT

DALLAS

The greatest work of art ever created by mankind. I will brook no argument there. If they'd had Dallas in the olden days, the Pope would have had it showing on the roof of the Sistine Chapel. And that's a medical fact.

DENTISTS

How can dentists' breath be so bad when all they think about all day is cleaning teeth? It's not like it can have slipped their minds. Are they too busy to actually do it?

Leaning over you and breathing mustard gas into your squinting face. Before I go to the dentist I make sure I've had a bag of pickled onion Monster Munch, a shook-up bottle of pop, a whole garlic clove and a filterless fag. Your first line of defence is attack.

Fig. 1
Dentist cocktail

DINOSAURS

Between Adam and Eve and Jesus, the world was full of dinosaurs. I don't know where the people were all that time. Probably hiding.

Dinosaurs were feckin' enormous and forever taking bites out of each other, and you want to be well clear of that. It'd be like sharing the place with a load of Mike Tysons with horns.

Then one day they all died out and nobody knows why. Now, I've got a theory, and unlike most of the feckin' rubbish Dermot picks up off the internet about Jamie Lee Curtis's secret truncheon, it's based on proper feckin' research.

Personally, I've seen three films on the subject: *Jurassic Parks*, *One of Our Dinosaurs Is Missing*, and another one where a Plasticine monster tries to pinch some poor lassie's tiger-skin bra, so I know what I'm talking about.

Your man Darwing worked this out: whoever has the most children wins. That passes for science in England. In Ireland, it's just basic feckin' observation. So, the big thing your dinosaurs need to do is breed. And if you've seen dinosaurs, they're not made for love, are they? All covered in spikes and the size of a feckin' church.

I've seen marriages founder 'cause the man puts on a few pounds or grows a moustache, and I'm sure men feel the same about their wives.

So the dinosaurs died out because they started doing whatever the dinosaur version is of rolling over at night and finishing that article in *The People's Friend* instead. Makes sense.

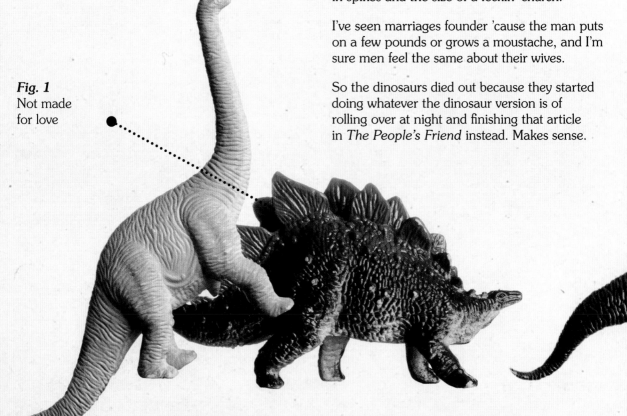

Fig. 1
Not made for love

And if you've seen the little arms on your Triannosaurus Rex, they wouldn't be able to find relief any other way, if you follow my drift. The poor feckers probably exploded.

Which explains why, when they find them, they're just little piles of bones.

There. What was so hard about that? I don't know what scientists do all day. Fill rabbits with shampoo, probably.

Fig. 2
No self-relieving with these tiny little hands

DREAMS

You can tell a lot about your life from your dreams. As far as I can tell, my life is a series of sausage-related bollocks that I sleep through half of. And that's not far off the truth.

But I've read all the articles in the magazines, and you get some funny interpretations. If you dream about teeth, it's to do with money. Why?

What have teeth got to do with money, except the feckin' cost of going to the dentist? And if you dream about being on a boat, it's about how your feelings are under control. I've dreamed about being on a boat once: when I fell asleep on the ferry from Dun Laoghaire. Now, call me simple, but I'm pretty sure I had a dream about being on a boat because I was on a feckin' boat.

You can keep all your superstitious mumbo-jumbo and New Age horseshite. Working out what your dreams are about is pretty simple.

Fig. 2
Interpreting your dreams:
a simple guide

What you're dreaming about	Meaning
Teeth	You're grinding your teeth. Or you've forgotten to take them out.
Going to the loo	You need the loo. Wake up before you piss the bed.
Being back at school	You went to school and you can still remember it.
Being chased	You know your leg fell off this afternoon? Well, it's just woken up without the rest of you.
Can't answer a question/ test	You won't admit it while you're awake, but you're not right about everything.
Car trouble	You own a feckin' car. What do you expect?
Being lost	You're not in your own bed.
Having sex	You're not.

Fig. 3
This actually works

Nightmares are a different kettle of fish. Nightmares are awful. Take Hilliary, for instance. She's a proper nightmare. She leaves me in a cold sweat, my heart going like the clappers, eyes staring like a madwoman.

I had a nightmare once that I'd never had any children. It was unreal. I dreamed I was one of Ireland's most successful businesswomen, running a worldwide greengrocery import-export business turning over more money than your fella from Dunnes. I was married to the lad from the front of the romantic novels with the chest like a chocolate bar, and I could fly anywhere at a moment's notice. And nobody needed a cup of tea, nobody wanted anything cleaned, nobody wanted my opinions on how to raise their babbies. It was feckin' awful.

I woke up drenched in sweat. Now I understand what Dermot meant when he was always after popping his sheets in the laundry because he'd had 'a wet dream' (see Laundry). I'd have shown him more sympathy if I'd known.

If you want a decent night's sleep, you need a mug of hot milk or a cocoa. (Bailey's in the microwave doesn't count, whatever Winnie might say.)

And they say if you want some exciting dreams, stuff a load of cheese down yourself before you go to bed. Didn't I believe that'd work? Night after night I've been getting through a packet of Wexford slices and a plate of crackers. It's done nothing for me except make me dream about having sausages, which is what I really wanted. And even when I've done the decent thing and gone to bed on a tummy full of sausages, I've only dreamed about having more sausages.

You know what? Those psychoticanalysts reckon they're so clever, but I bet if you looked up in one of those Sigmund Fraud books what dreaming about a sausage means, there wouldn't be anything in it.

You're not poking around in my subcontinent, looking for dirt. Sometimes a sausage is just a sausage.

IS FOR...

BEWARE

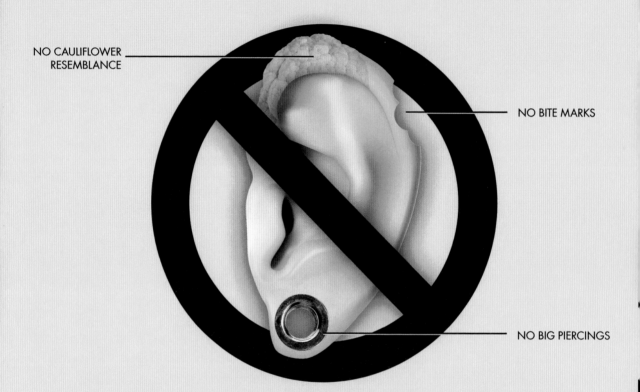

NO CAULIFLOWER RESEMBLANCE

NO BITE MARKS

NO BIG PIERCINGS

EARS

You can tell if someone's a weirdo by their ears. It's saved this family a whole barrel-load of grief with Cathy's potential boyfriends. No point ending up with a babby that looks like a darts trophy. They need two of them for a start. They mustn't be too close together or flapping about like taxi doors. They should be in a straight line, one each side. And if they must look like a cauliflower, it should be the leaves, not the scrunched-up brainy bit. If one of them's been bit off or pierced with anything bigger than a split pea, that's your warning to steer clear.

ESCALATORS

Take an up escalator, fine. At my age, you'll take any free ride you can get, whether it's from a man or a machine. I'm not picky. But if you can't be arsed to walk downstairs, you might as well crawl into a 6-foot hole and pull the mud over.

I saw a sign on an escalator once: dogs must be carried. Took me half an hour to find one. That's not true, that's a joke. I promised Ginger Balls I'd put one in.

volution

Once upon a time, we were all Adam's children. Now, apparently, we're all bald chimps. Well, I must say, as I look around, I can see why your man Darwing came to that conclusion. I've seen people round Temple Bar who look like they still live up trees and scratch each other for pleasure.

What your man Darwing said was that the clever monkeys left the other monkeys behind, jumped out of the trees and came down for a look around. Down here, they found they looked a lot cleverer if they stood up, so they stood up. Pretty soon they let a lot of their hair fall out so they could look cleverer. And then they started eating properly, instead of stuffing their faces with bananas.

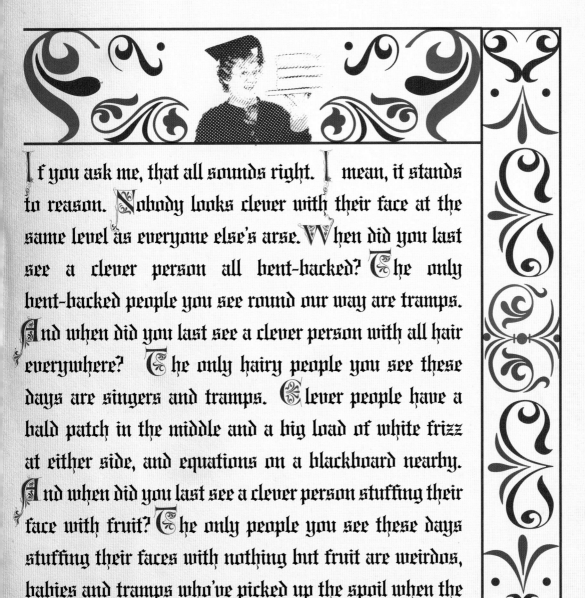

If you ask me, that all sounds right. I mean, it stands to reason. Nobody looks clever with their face at the same level as everyone else's arse. When did you last see a clever person all bent-backed? The only bent-backed people you see round our way are tramps. And when did you last see a clever person with all hair everywhere? The only hairy people you see these days are singers and tramps. Clever people have a bald patch in the middle and a big load of white frizz at either side, and equations on a blackboard nearby. And when did you last see a clever person stuffing their face with fruit? The only people you see these days stuffing their faces with nothing but fruit are weirdos, babies and tramps who've picked up the spoil when the market's finished on a Saturday.

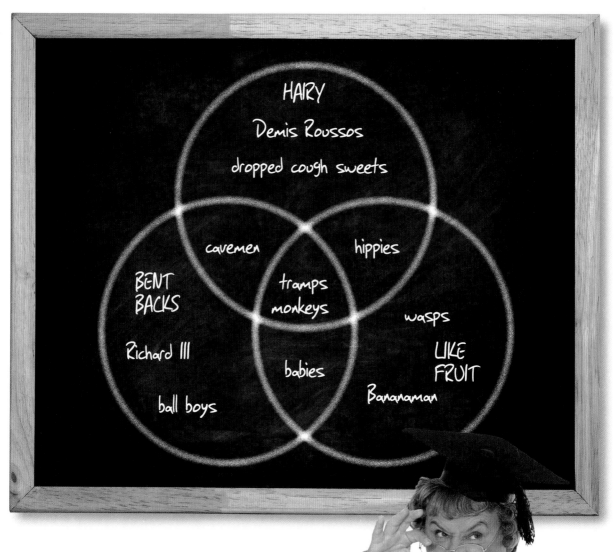

HAIRY
Demis Roussos
dropped cough sweets

cavemen   hippies

BENT
BACKS   tramps
               monkeys   wasps

Richard III   LIKE
                                FRUIT

               babies
                          Bananaman
ball boys

That's it: monkeys are basically tramps.

But – BUT BUT BUT – there's another thing. Your tramp – he's a man, right? Your hairy singer – he's a man, right? Your weirdo – he's a man, right? Who's never a tramp or a hairy singer or a weirdo? Us girls, that's who.

Us girls – with no beards, and somewhere to sleep, and a proper feckin' diet of sausages – we're the most evolved of the lot. We're the ones who mash bananas for the babbies. We're the ones who dole out soup to the tramps. We're the ones who manage to stand bolt upright even when we're carrying 5lbs of extra weight hanging off our poor shoulders.

Adam, my arse.

We're all Eve's children. Eve was the clever one. She wasn't covered in hair and hunched up. She'd never have reached that apple if she couldn't stand up properly. An apple she didn't even want, because she's not a bendy-over great furry thing with all fruit in her beard.

They say Adam made Eve from his rib. Did he bollix. That's just a man taking credit for a woman, as per feckin' usual. I bet he said he was making her, and was really just hiding in the shed, pretending to be busy, sneaking a gasper and reading mucky books, coming in every so often with a pencil behind his ear to recharge his drill, just so he looked busy. The crafty fecker. I bet Eve made herself. A self-made woman. I know how that feels.

What I'm saying is: monkeys are tramps, and tramps are men. The ones who bothered to evolve are the women. And all credit to your man Darwing – who had a shocker of a beard, and was probably bent double from all the scurvy (the poor fella had to eat a tortoise at one point) – he pointed it out. It's no wonder he was unpopular in his day. He had the guts to say it: women have turned into the clever ones; men are still basically chimps.

Evolution's dead easy to understand.

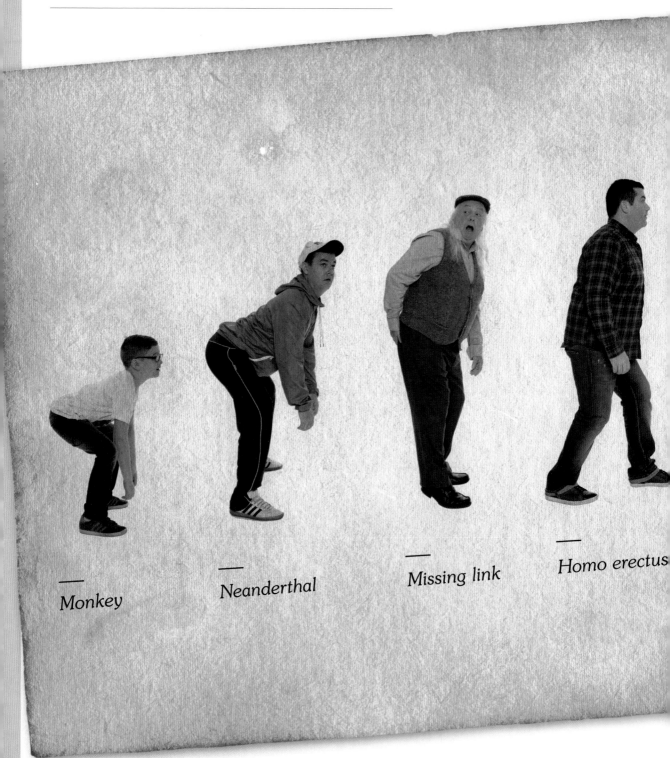

Monkey

Neanderthal

Missing link

Homo erectus

Homo sapien

Buster Brady

Chimp

Fig. 1
Darwing's famous
'seven stages of Man'

IS FOR...
FECKIN'
FALLING
OVER &
FECKIN'
FAMOUS
PEOPLE

FALLING OVER

Back in the good old days, people were always falling over. What a lovely sight it was. People slipping and tumbling and going flat on their arses. They were happy times. You knew if a person was funny by the way they fell over. And you could tell a good film from a waste of a bag of chips because in the good ones your man fell over. More than once.

These days, you just don't see people falling over nearly as much. Maybe it's because we've got better shoes now. Or clever pavements. And we're all safety mad. Look at the feckin' railings round everything. Winnie reckons she saw a bunch of daffodils with railings round them the other week. Mind you, they never did get all that cataract out.

The greats of falling over are all gone now, sadly. Buster Keaton. Charlie Chaplin. George Best. These days the youngsters aren't interested in falling over. Sure, they don't mind staggering a bit – but you won't catch them going heels up and rump down. Face-down on a Friday night, maybe, twisted on blue vodka-pop. But that's not how you fall over.

Sure, I don't know what they teach kids at drama school these days* but it isn't good old-fashioned falling over. Perhaps they need an *X Factor* equivalent for falling over. Or something like *The Voice*. They could call it *The Arse*.

---

*How to fan their fuckin' faces with their hands, as far as I can tell. You don't fool me, you gobshites. You're not really crying.

This is how you fall over:

1 First – on your arse, never your face. There's a reason there's all that padding behind you.

2 If you're doing it from ground level, make it a good, flat-footed slip. Heel up, high-kick, look to the side.

3 Try to get your balance back with a bit of flapping.

4 Make a lot of 'whoooaaahhh' noises.

5 Tumble backwards neatly, still flapping and whoooaaahhhing.

6 When you hit the ground, stay there a moment. Soak up the love.

7 Sit up and pull a face.

THE HOTTEST Z-LIST MUM'S GOSSIP MAGAZ

mammy's

SPECIAL HOME COOKING ISSUE

INSIDE

**U-TUBE EXCLUSIVE
BACKSTAGE INTERVIEW
& MAUREEN NOLAN:
HOW TO GET FAMOUS
IN 5 MINUTES**

EXCLUSIVE
MRS BROWN'S
SAUSAGE SECRETS

DETTOL
WITH EV

WHAT THE?! WEI
VEG ON PAGE 55

*early-onset
demerera*

94

I'VE NEVER FECKIN' HEARD OF ANY OF THEM.

I know they're famous, because they're all over the magazines and in those things on TV that they only let famous people in, like quizzes and the news, but I've no idea who any of them are.

I thought it was that early-onset demerera, but I've asked down the hairdresser's and nobody knows who any of them are. I bet some of them don't even know who they are themselves.

I mean, I say nobody knows but Rory seems to be able to put a name to all the faces. But then, because nobody's heard of them, I don't know if he's just making them up. Some of the names seem a bit feckin' far-fetched, if you ask me. Agyness. Well, her Mammy obviously couldn't spell. Shia? Do me a favour. Sounds like someone trying not to swear (see Swearing). And I don't believe anyone's ever been christened Puff since that feckin' magic dragon on all the drugs.

Not that there aren't still famous people I've heard of. I've heard of me, and I suppose, in a way, I'm famous.

I've been on the tellybox, have a very successful market stall and my opinions on important matters of the day are widely sought after (see Laundry), so in many ways I'm no different to household names like Bongo Whatshisname with the sunglasses from the band U-Tube, or Pierce Bronson, or Dettol.

But still, the way I see it, I'm a Mammy who happens to be a famous person, not a famous person who happens to be a Mammy. I know which side my job is buttered and it's family first, fans second. I learned this valuable lesson from the lovely Evelyn Cusack, the weather lady off the telly. She was busy giving me an autograph once when I turned round too quickly and knocked her daughter into a pond. And if she'd been paying more attention to her family and less to her fans, that awful thing would never have happened.

Above: Re-enactment of the unhappy child in pond

Sure you get bothered sometimes, for a photo or a stain removal tip, but I say being famous, every head turning when you enter the Sue Ryder shop, is no different than being a very beautiful woman, and I've borne that burden with dignity for many years.

I feel for the poor famous people nobody's heard of. They must be fierce confused, sometimes, not quite knowing who they are or why anyone's after sticking a camera up their knickers when they get out of a car.

I blame the people who decide who's famous. Whoever they might be. The feckin' eejits. They obviously don't know what they're doing, choosing the parade of numpties they pick. If I had my way, the following famous people, proper famous people, would be famous, and no one else, unless they'd passed an exam.

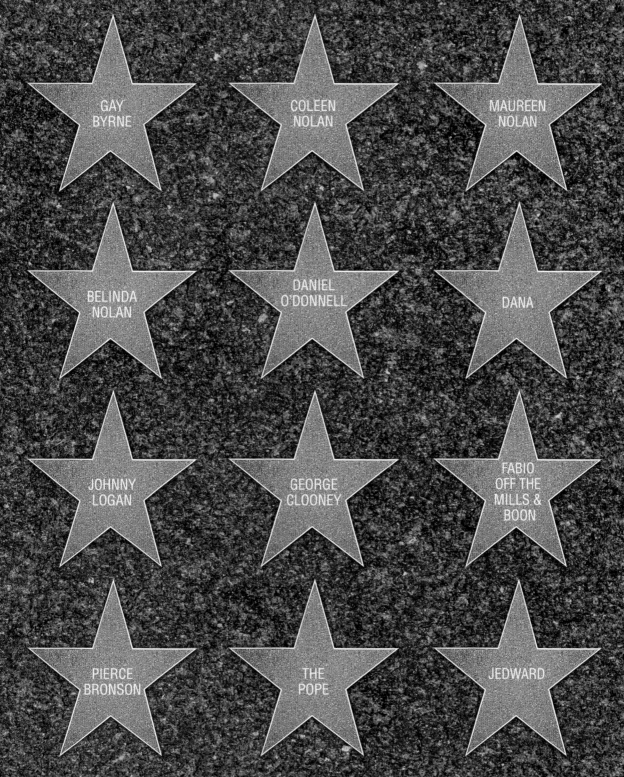

GAY BYRNE

COLEEN NOLAN

MAUREEN NOLAN

BELINDA NOLAN

DANIEL O'DONNELL

DANA

JOHNNY LOGAN

GEORGE CLOONEY

FABIO OFF THE MILLS & BOON

PIERCE BRONSON

THE POPE

JEDWARD

And the trouble is that people will do *anything* to become famous. They'll film themselves having a bunk up. They'll eat a kangaroo's willy. They'll go out draped from head to toe in nothing but bacon. There was one lad I saw on the telly wearing a feckin' dress and a wig and woman's make-up.

looking like a cross between Barbara Cartland and a toilet-roll cosy, and they gave him a feckin' award for scribbling all over a flowerpot. Imagine that. Giving an award to some fella on the TV dressed up as a woman! The whole world's feckin' crackers.

IS FOR...
GHOSTS, GLASSES, GM FOOD AND GOING TO THE TOILET DURING THE NIGHT

GHOSTS

Winnie says she saw the ghost of her Jacko hanging round the landing one night, putting up some shelves he'd promised to get round to in 1988. She was terribly fussed – she thought he'd passed away in the ward – but when she phoned, he was fine. I said his ghost was probably just getting started early. He's got so much unfinished business, it can't wait till he's dead.

GLASSES

I only wear glasses for seeing. Someone told me I should get laser eye surgery, but laser eyes can do terrible damage. I've seen it in the cartoons. I can give a look that would turn milk to yoghurt without needing to cut sheet metal in half.

I've got a pair of reading glasses, and a pair of what I call 'distance ones', because they're always miles from where I think I've left them. If you can't find your glasses, try putting them on a chain, because that's more uncomfortable to sit on.

Last time I was turning the house upside down for my readers, Cathy told me lots of women my age switch to bifocals, but I've never really fancied a woman and I'm not sure what we'd do in bed; besides, this sort of smutty talk wasn't getting my feckin' glasses found.

GM FOOD

I don't agree with all this tinkering with food, Geriatrically Modifying it to make it look fresher and less wrinkly. It's not right. I ate raisins for years and never worried they were funny-looking. Then science turns them all smooth, Geriatrically Modifies them to look younger, and suddenly we've got 'grapes'. What the feck are they playing at? It's not natural. What would you think if you bit into a bun and found a grape? You'd call the police. I know I have.

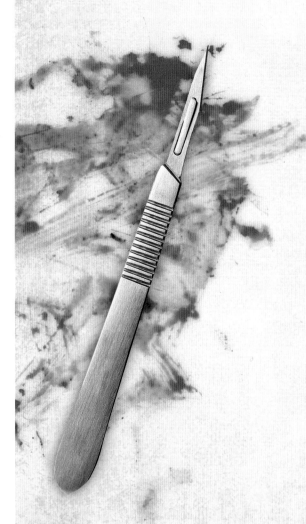

GOING TO THE TOILET DURING THE NIGHT

There are times when you can't wait. Usually on buses. Or during weddings. (God knows they go on a bit, especially if the bride's parents insist on the full-fat mass, instead of the nice semi-skimmed one that you can whip through in an hour.)

The biggest threat to a Mammy's bladder comes during the night. Sure, a big mug of milky Horlicks gets you to sleep, but when it comes knocking at your exit in the wee hours (and we all know how they got their name), you have to let the thing out, like a cat.

If you're at home, all well and good – you can just slip to the bathroom, get your business out of the way and get back under the covers.

But then there's the complications.

❶ WHAT IF THERE'S SOMEONE STAYING?

House guests are a bastard nuisance.

They're in an unfamiliar bed, so they don't sleep well, so the slightest little noise is going to wake them up. I've laid dead still some nights when there's someone staying, for fear that if I turn over, the creak of the bedsprings is going to make them think I'm doing the sort of thing Winnie gets the giggles about after her first couple of drinks. Filthy cow.

And you can't even use a bedpan – if you've even got one. And I'm lucky my Mammy left me one in her will. (It was empty, before you ask. Apart from a dead spider.) Feck knows where you buy a bedpan these days. Probably in the chemist's, on that shelf with all the specialist stuff, like man pads and nappies for Gran. And that's officially

The Last Place You Ever Want To Be Feckin' Seen, believe me.

The problem with a bedpan is that you might as well piddle into a gong. People three streets away will know you're going. Some will probably get their coats on for church. So forget the bedpan.

Your best weapon in the war of bladder v. house guest is a seriously soft pair of slippers. I've got some that look like a pair of ducks. Perfect. Like wearing a couple of trifles. You could Lambada over landmines wearing them and come away in one piece.

The other thing you need is a good mental map of where your squeaky floorboards are. I know mine: there's The Creaker, at the top of the stairs, The Cracker, next to the radiator on the landing, and That Feckin' Floorboard, right in front of the bedroom door. I have to take a leap of faith over that one. And a quick one. The last thing you need when you're carrying a full bladder is to have to do the splits.

D'PISSY WEE WEE

Then there's the act itself. If you're canny, you can sit at a funny angle so it all goes on the side of the pan and doesn't splash noisily into the water. I've worked out my angle: leaning over, left hand on the far side of the sink, right leg up on the bin. It's not a pretty sight, true. But this isn't a spectator sport. It's a stealth mission. It's like trying to free a hostage made of piss.

Then there's the question your man Shakespeare asked: to flush or not to flush? Well, he'd obviously given it no feckin' thought whatsoever. Of course you don't feckin' flush. Do you want to undo all your good work, and have your house guest up and about at 5.20 a.m.? (It is always 5.20 a.m. you need a pee, isn't it? Right when it's exactly too early to get up. If it was 5.30, you could always say you didn't want to miss the best part of the day. But at 5.20, it might as well be feckin' midnight. I mean, you see Mammies queuing for the corner shop to open at 5.30, to get the papers early or stock up on tea, but no Mammy in her right mind would be standing outside the newsagent's at 5.20. She'd be moved on as a tramp.)

② WHAT TO DO WHEN YOU'RE AWAY FROM HOME

So you're staying in a B&B, or a hotel, if you're posh. Now the stakes are a whole lot feckin' higher. A mental map's not good enough this time. You need a real map. So pack a paper and pencil.

You've seen those things they put on TV at the end of the night when they've run out of programmes, haven't you? The ones designed to put the shits up you right when you're about to go to bed. There's one about knowing your exit route if your house caught fire. It's bucking terrifying, so it is, but it's not real: *it's code.* Any Mammy knows which direction to head if the house is on fire: wherever the nice hunk of a fireman is heading.

No, that little programme is the TV's way of making you think about your route to the bathroom when you're away from home.

So, first things first, get to know your territory. Ask for a look around before you say yes to the room. If the bathroom's more than one landing away, forget it. If you've got to go past more than a couple of doors, forget it. Ideally, you want the room but one next to the bathroom: not next to the bathroom, because the sound of everybody else peeing and flushing will keep you awake half the night. Especially the fellas, who are basically competing to see who can be the loudest. Some of them sound like an elephant pissing into a lift shaft.

Once you've got your room, practise your route. Draw it on your paper, marking any creaky hotspots. Then learn the layout of the bathroom — ESPECIALLY WHERE THE LOCK IS. The lock is your first and only line of defence against other holidaymakers (and we all like a drink when we're away from home) busting in on you and catching you wiping your fritter.

Next, do a couple of practice runs. Tread softly. See if you can do it in complete silence. Think of it as learning a lifesaving dance routine. Step, step, step. Then, once you've got it, try it with your eyes shut. If anyone catches you at this point, tell them you're having a migraine or you got caught short in the middle of a prayer.

Now you should be ready. You might also be half an hour late for dinner. But balls to being on time. Dignity is nine-tenths of the law. Besides, you'll drink less if you're late to the dining room, and that'll help.

One last thing: set your alarm. Set it for 5.15. The last thing you want is to be caught in the rush-hour scramble at 5.20. It's all very well meeting your fellow holidaymakers, but not while you're all in your nighties with your knees clamped together.

REMEMBER: If you do piss the bed, grab a toddler out of one of the kids' rooms, say you heard them having a nightmare. Drag them into bed with you half asleep, and in the morning, pin the blame on them.

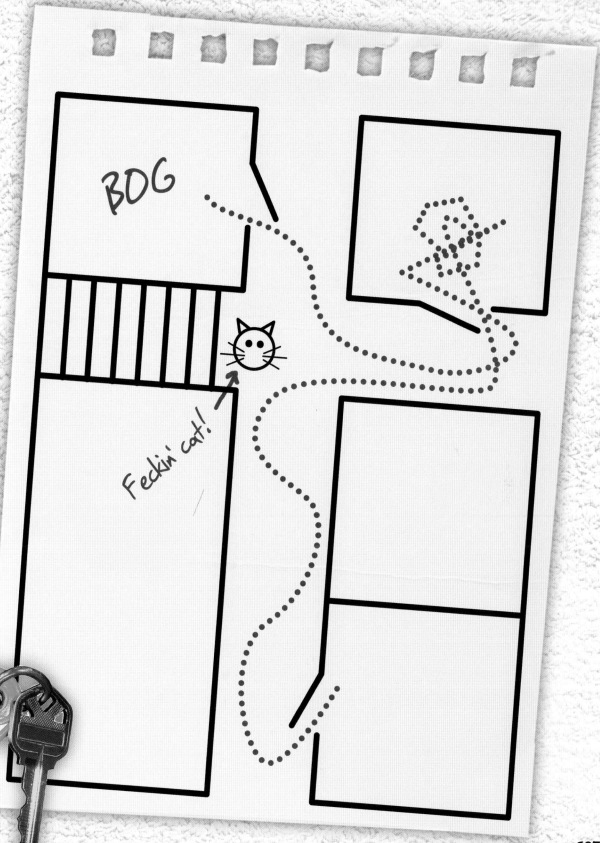

BOG

Feckin cat!

IS FOR...

HAIR

Hair is weird when you think about it.

I've been thinking about hair now for more than twenty minutes and I didn't notice I'd burned some spaghetti hoops on the hob and I'm going to be most of the afternoon soaking them off and Grandad's going to have to have Toast Toppers again and they go through him like the feckin' Eurostar and stain the pan worse than piccalilli. And that's how weird hair is.

Unless you're Goldilocks Brogan, who runs the veg stall by the Lidl end of the market, with his head all shiny and pink and little wispy bits poking up like he was a walking radish, you'll have hair.

Hair is the bit of your body that keeps growing, and that means you can go and make it into different colours and shapes to show it off. And if you make a giant feckin' twerp of yourself, you can just hack it all away and wait for a new lot.

Imagine if that happened with your hands. Great big hands, all primped, or permed, or pinned back, with streaks in. 'You're not going out with your hands like that, young lady.' 'Ooh, I love what you've done with your hands, Agnes.' 'I just washed my hands and I can't do a thing with them.' It beggars the imagination.

But look at me. I'm wandering off the subject.

Or arses. Imagine that. If your arse kept growing. Great big arses, all carefully washed with Pentapeptibollocks and Hallo Vera and Jojojobo to make them extra shiny. Lads with their bum all scruffed up fashionable with arse wax. There are those monkeys who look like they've let their arse grow out and given it a pillar-box-red dye job to show off, but (a) I'm not 100 per cent sure it's the same thing, and (2) I'm not typing 'monkey bum' into Cathy's tablet to find out, because they cater to all sorts of perverts on the internet now. You should see some of the shocking pictures popped up when I did a Google to find out the name of that bleeding arsehole off the news. I still see that screen when I close my eyes, like a haunted doctor.

Hair grows mainly on the head (unless you're Goldilocks Brogan, where it grows mainly on your onions), but also on the legs, armpits, face and as decoration for the downstairs entrances, to make them look nice, a bit like the pot plants they have in the foyers of swanky hotels.

HAIRCUTS

Like many women my age, I no longer bother with the undignified to-ing and fro-ing of fashion.

I found a hairstyle that worked for me and have stuck with it, like Jennifer Aniston, or Brian May. I get it done every two weeks, to maintain the shape, and I style it using that gold stuff that's had the same picture on the tin since before the miniskirt was invented. It's a look and I'm not changing. You should be able to identify a lady of a certain age by her trademark silhouette, like people do with planes. The only way I'm likely to change my hairstyle now is if I'm swapping a fuse and accidentally stick my finger in that hole under the box where the mouse chewed through the cables.

22 Ultimate bad hair days

Bad hair day? *The haircuts you wish never happened*

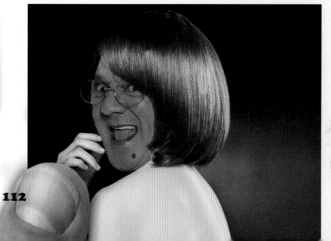

112

They say you should always go to the hair saloon with a picture of how you want it cut. Well, I don't need one. I just point in the mirror and say, 'Like that.'

Miriam, who does my hair at 'Wash 'n' Blow' (the boutique formerly known as 'Hairy Styles', formerly 'Lady Dye', formerly 'Scissor Act', formerly 'Brush Hour', formerly 'Hair T'riffic Control', formerly 'Chop-Along-Cassidy', formerly 'Hair To-dye, Comb Tomorrow', formerly 'Snip, Cra-curl and Bob', formerly 'Curl-dye-locks and the Free Hairs', formerly 'Scissor Act 2: Back in the Habit', formerly 'Heady or Knot, Hair I Comb', formerly 'Hairy Trimportant Permson', formerly 'The Hairdresser's'), respects someone who makes a decision and sticks to it, so I leave myself in her capable hands.

In the past, I've been nagged by some sillybollix trainee snipper with *no idea of the consequences* into trying some radical change of hairdo, and I look back now at the God-awful results of these foolish experiments with nothing but regret, a bit like those lads who stuck that ear to the back of a mouse. It's not pretty.

Perm *(1976)*

I took in a picture of Michael Jackson singing, and I think they copied the squashy bit on top of the microphone instead.

Fringe *(1983)*

Dreadful. Looked like I'd taken a hat off I'd been wearing all winter.

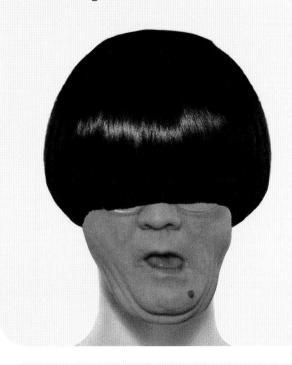

Beehive *(1992)*

Hairdresser said this was retro. Lost three combs, constantly hoovering hair off the top jamb of the kitchen doorway. Disaster.

Britney *(2007)*

No idea what I was feckin' thinking here, but in my defence they were doing three for two on this ferocious Belgian cider down Foley's. Dark times.

Women are under constant pressure to change their hair, especially for a big bash.

On Betty's wedding day, she'd had so many little ringlets and fancy whatnots done to her hair, Mark didn't recognize her. When the whole ceremony's about being faithful to one person, I think it's a bad idea to turn up looking like someone else. Might give him the wrong idea.

Men, on the other hand, have a choice of two hairstyles (unless they're Goldilocks Brogan, in which case they have a choice of two hats):

1 The Proper Bloody Haircut

For upstanding, trustworthy members of society, architects, doctors, strippers, etc., who can often be found at events giving talks with slides or signing the back of other people's passport photos.

2 The Hippy

For antisocial layabouts who don't care about getting a decent job.

HAIRDRYERS

If, God forbid, there's a volcano – and don't rule it out, we had hail and sunshine at the same time yesterday, it's all gone crazy since we got that new orzone layer put in – and robot archolologists from the future dig my house out from the rocks and try to work out what life was like from the valuable goods I was buried with, like they did with that Egyptian fella, they'll think we worshipped hairdryers. I've got dozens of the feckers.

And the thing about hairdryers I've noticed is that none of them work, except the big ones you pull over your head like a crash helmet down the hair saloon. I keep buying different ones, asking for new ones for Christmas and birthdays, and Buster's found me loads off the back of this lorry that keeps passing his house, but I can't find one that works like the astronaut helmet. I think that one's best because you can fall asleep under it. The droning noise sends me off. And then the smell of burning hair wakes you up. It's a design classic.

In a drawer under my bed, I've got all the attachments for hairdryers I've ever owned. I've no idea what possible use they are, but I find it oddly comforting to know they're there. A bit like Winnie is with her Jacko.

1
Six of these things that look like the front of a frightening deep-sea fish, though now I look at them, one of them might be a hoover attachment and one's a squashed shoe. Never used.

2
Eight of these shower attachment things. Could be for pasta or dreadlocks. Never used.

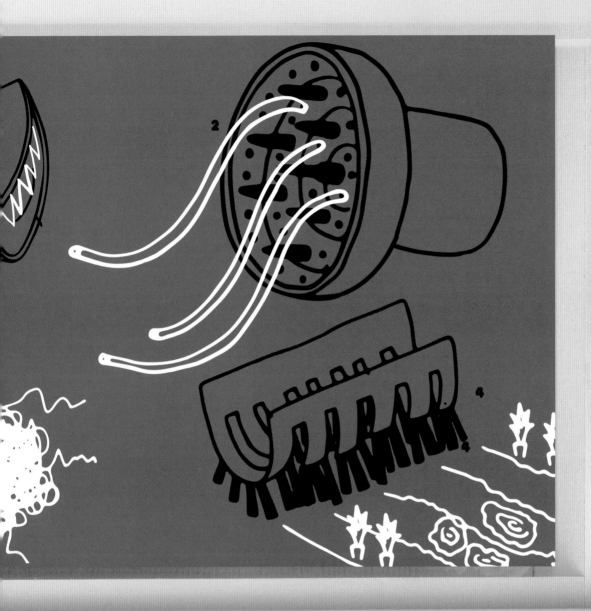

3

Eleven of these things that are a cross between a comb and a hand, sort of what Edward Scissorhands would have if he was Edward Combhands, if that makes sense. Have used one of these once but it got caught and I had to brush a hump of hair over it until Miriam could cut it out.

4

Sixteen of these. A kind of plough attachment, like they drag on the back of a tractor, but for hair. Useful if you haven't got a brush, but what kind of eejit's got two dozen hairdryers and no brush? Pointless. Never used except on dog and Grandad.

HANDWRITING

Nobody writes anything down any more. They're all doing stuff on their phones with their thumbs.

In a million years we'll just be a big thumb, the rest of the body withered to a little pink raisin thing, and what good's that for anything but hitch-hiking and pushing in drawing pins? I don't want to live in a world like that, and I'm glad I'll be long gone.

I myself have beautiful handwriting. Cathy says it's like a spider has crawled across the page. Which is a real compliment, because if you've seen some of the webs those clever little beggars turn out, they're really something. And you've heard about the money people get paid for being web designers these days? Jaysus. It's obviously quite a skill.

I mainly use my handwriting for:

Greetings cards

Shopping lists

Angry notes to leave under windscreen wipers when people park their Range Rover on the feckin' pavement outside Dunnes so I can't get my wheelie trolley past

The last of those is mainly underlining, but stylish penwork gets your point across more clearly than shouting, or violence. Truly, as Oscar Wild (our old milkman) said, the pen is mightier than a knee in the knackers.

It's important that your handwriting isn't just beautiful, but also clear. Cross the t's and dot the i's and mind your p's and q's. And mind you don't fall flat on your r's.

Handwriting should be clear and readable, especially to yourself.

Otherwise you can get in the most terrible trouble shopping. Even with my expert penmanship, the number of times I've bought a load of bread instead of a loaf. Filled the freezer up till there was no room for sausages. And then there was the time with the crap sticks. And the greasy poof paper. And those two tits of rice padding. I don't even know what ebbs are, but I wasted a whole morning looking for a dozen of them down the supermarket. I guess we'll never know.

The people with the worst handwriting are doctors. I always check any prescriptions I get given, in case the handwriting can be misread. (Because you never know when you might get a lucky '200 Valium' scribble.) If it's something I need, though, I make sure the pharmacist knows exactly what's wrong with me by sneezing it over them first.

The one place it is fine to let your handwriting get a bit slapdash is on a Christmas card where you can't for the life of you remember their kids' names.

A sloppy hand covers a multitude of sins. As I told Dermot once when I found him reading mucky books under his duvet.

Season's greetings

To Helen and Victor, Gdohat,
Dswmes and little Bbonbtny

We must meet up
soon!

Love from

Agnes, Rodser, Mark,
Rorg, Trevor, Coxhy,
Ddoftqrk and baby Dtlopw

X X X

VALUE CHARITY CARDS

SALE NOW ONLY
£0.02P

HEARING AIDS

They have these invisible ones now they advertise in the supplements. That's the last feckin' thing you need when you're getting on a bit. You can't hear a thing, and now you've been given something you can't see. They used to come in one colour: Elastoplast. They were so big, it looked like you were on the phone, and they were made of the same stuff. At least people gave you some respect that way. With an invisible one, they'll think you're just being rude.

But if you turn them up loud enough and cup your hand to your ear, you can make a noise that attracts dogs, which is handy if you're feeling lonely in the park.

HEDGEHOGS

Where have they all gone? Wasn't I only saying the other day to Winnie, time was when I'd leave a little bowl of milk by the shed.

Most nights there'd be a cute little fella lapping away at me dish.

(I'm still talking about hedgehogs. Don't get carried away.) But that was then. Now you couldn't find a hedgehog with a hedgehog magnet.*

And is there anybody making a fuss about this? Is there feck. Sure, it's fine to whine about your whales and your tigers and your pandas – all enormous feckin' creatures, most of which would probably kill you if you left them a saucer of milk by the shed – but no one seems to be sticking up for the poor little hoggie.

Well, that's where I come in.

I've worked out where the poor blighters are going. It's obvious when you think about it.

You've seen all those skinny-arsed sniper's nightmares flouncing around Hollywood in the magazines, haven't you? All fake bake and $50,000 frocks and legs like strands of spaghetti and bucking great handbags? More feckin' money than sense. More feckin' make-up than body fat. It's them. I'm telling you.

Because what have they all got in their dirty great bags? Little teeny-weeny doggies. Tiny pups. 'Aw, isn't he cute, so? Little furry fella.' Isn't he, though? But wait a minute – when did you ever see a dog you could sit in the palm of your hand? Science doesn't make dogs that small. Dogs are wolves. Mother Nature's got no need for miniature wolves. The others'd eat them.

*Note: put that one in the section on 'Priorities for Science', if I get time to put that in the book. Actually, I should make a list of these. Things I ought to put in the book. Only I'd lose it with the shopping lists and stuff on the fridge. Maybe I could get Cathy to put a little reminder thing that could go off on her computer pad. What are they called? A Napp. Right, put 'inventing a Napp that reminds me to make a list of things for the book including Priorities for Science' on that list of Priorities for Science I was talking about. There. Job done.

Ah, but Agnes, I can hear you say, Mother Nature doesn't need miniature trees either, and look what the Japanese have done with their bonzo gardens.

Exactly. Man-made interference. And I'm telling you, as sure as my name's Agnes Brown, those mini-dogs the starlets are poncing around with are poor little hedgehogs who've had their spikes removed by some cruel bastard in a white coat so they can be sold on as little pets.

That's where the hedgehogs have gone: Hollywood. And they're being made to perform naked. It's disgusting.

HOLLYWOOD

HISTORY

They say that if you don't know history, you're doomed to repeat it.

That's certainly what happened to Dermot. Twice he resat that exam, and he'd still be there if he hadn't been offered the job on the bacon counter.

By the way, some people give you a famous quote like that and don't tell you who said it. Not me.

I can give you chapter and verse: it was Winnie. She was reading it off a beer mat down Foley's. And it's that sort of thorough feckin' research that makes this book better than any rubbish you'll read on the so-called World Why-Web.

The Magnus Carter

History might seem like it's none of your business, but it's not all treaties and people you've never heard of, like Magnus Carter; every family has history, the tales that make us who we are. If you've got a story you tell about Grandad getting trapped crotch-first in the hairy brush thing in the letterbox, you've got history. Sure, a story like that might not be something you can turn into an essay that'll pass you an exam, as Dermot kept finding out, but it's as good as any dusty old book in the Dublin library.

So I say it pays to know where you came from, even if it's just to stop you getting jumped-up ideas about yourself (mentioning no names, Hilliary Nicolson, with your great-grandfather who used to push a cart full of dead dogs through the streets, and that's a fact because I saw it even though you covered it up with your hand when you were showing me that laminated sheet you'd had done about your family history, and you were pointing at the Victorian fella who'd designed that post office). History _does not lie_.

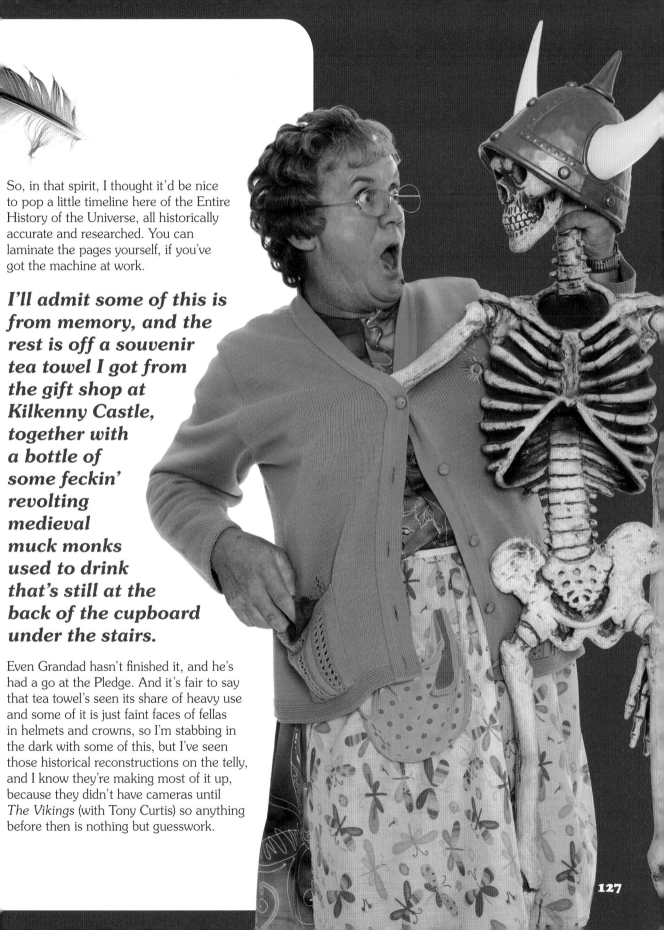

So, in that spirit, I thought it'd be nice to pop a little timeline here of the Entire History of the Universe, all historically accurate and researched. You can laminate the pages yourself, if you've got the machine at work.

I'll admit some of this is from memory, and the rest is off a souvenir tea towel I got from the gift shop at Kilkenny Castle, together with a bottle of some feckin' revolting medieval muck monks used to drink that's still at the back of the cupboard under the stairs.

Even Grandad hasn't finished it, and he's had a go at the Pledge. And it's fair to say that tea towel's seen its share of heavy use and some of it is just faint faces of fellas in helmets and crowns, so I'm stabbing in the dark with some of this, but I've seen those historical reconstructions on the telly, and I know they're making most of it up, because they didn't have cameras until *The Vikings* (with Tony Curtis) so anything before then is nothing but guesswork.

THE ENTIRE HISTORY
OF THE UNIVERSE

Ages Ago
Big bang. Terrible feckin' racket, like the bins being done, but worse. God woken up by noise, grumpy, wishing he'd given the feckin' thing a 'snooze' button.

ROAR!

Dinosaur Times
Dinosaurs feckin' everywhere.

1,000,000 Years BC
War between humans and dinosaurs ends with defeat for dinosaurs. Dinosaurs put arms 'beyond use'. They were tiny and not much use anyway.

A Little After That
God has a poo and brushes His hair. Gets down to work.

A Bit Later
Moon invented. Mainly rocks. Running out of ideas now.

A Fair While Back Now
Earth invented. Trees and animals, waterfalls, rainbows and that. Good start.

7500 BC
First settlers land in Ireland. Civilization begins.

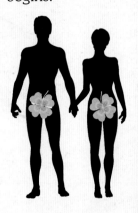

Greek Times
Greeks feckin' everywhere.

Feck off!

My headgear is better than your headgear.

Roman Times
Romans feckin' everywhere. They made a big fuss, but it's the Greeks again, really.

1014
Battle of Clontarf, between, apparently, a ghost with a moustache and a piss-coloured outline (might be a tea stain).

Egyptian Times
Pyramids and so on. For more details, ask Cathy or Winnie, who were both handmaidens of Cleopatra in a previous life, according to that lady who had the tent in the arcade. As was Dermot, so I suspect she's not to be trusted.

432 AD
St Patrick brings Christianity to Ireland, frightens snakes away and celebrates his own day by getting mortal in a big green felt hat shaped like a pint of mead.

Viking Times
Vikings feckin' everywhere, including Ireland: lots of rape and porridge (at least on tea towel).

THE ENTIRE HISTORY OF THE UNIVERSE CONTINUED...

1541
Henry VIII declares himself King of Ireland, a bit like when Grandad wakes up in the middle of the night swearing he's Elton John.

1692
Penal laws. Catholics banned from doing anything fun except having kids and drinking. Law not repealed until 1829, though spirit of law still observed.

1649
Cromwell lands in Ireland. Exact location uncertain (hole in tea towel).

1858
Patent for first rotary washing machine.

1892
Invention of the spin-dryer.

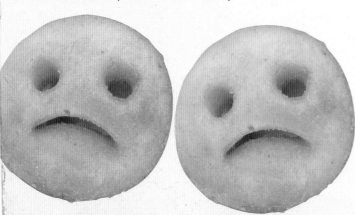

1845
Potato famine. Horrendous affair. Whole nation faint for lack of chips.

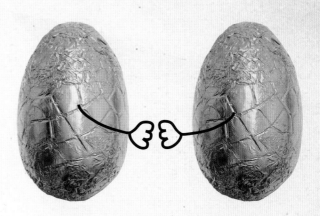

1919
Anglo-Irish War. Britain gets to keep the top bit, Ireland gets the rest. If you did that with a carrot, it'd be clear who'd won.

Britain

Ireland

1990
Mary Robinson first woman president of Ireland with a beard and glasses, though this may be permanent marker.

1998
Good Friday Agreement. Can't remember what this was all about. Might be something to do with Easter eggs.

1984
Daniel O'Donnell's first album, *The Boy from Donegal*, released. According to Winnie, who won a socket set at a pub quiz with that fact.

1949
Irish Republic declared. Faint trace of tomato ketchup.

IS FOR ME
(SEE FRONT COVER)

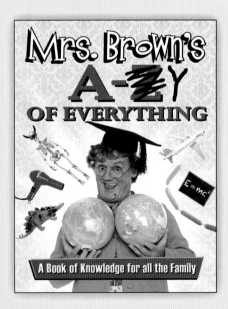

IS FOR...
A COUPLE
OF THINGS

JAMES JOYCE

Wonderful pub. Does pies with enormous meaty lumps and proper bottoms (see Pies). Reminds me of that DVD Rory left in the player once.

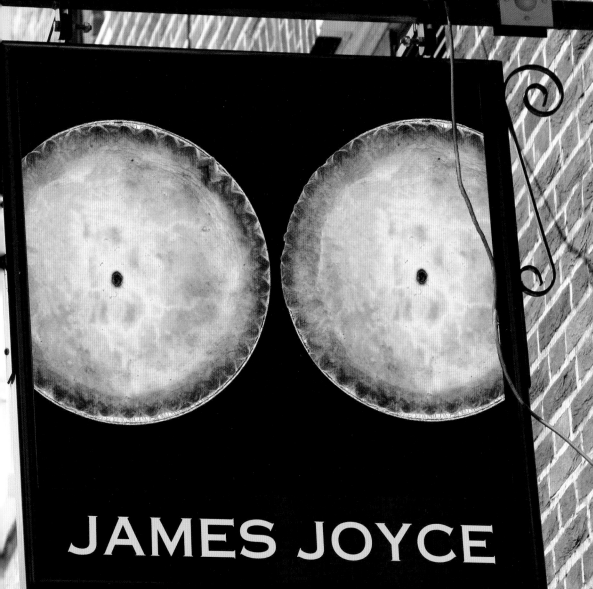

JAMES JOYCE

WE SERVE PIES
WITH PROPER BOTTOMS

137

WEDDING
MEMORIES

JIGSAWS

Don't spend money on shop-bought ones. You can make your own out of the box of wedding photos that get cut up and put in the loft. Or pair people off with celebrities out of the magazines. Hours of fun.

IS FOR...

KARATE

Trevor's friend Squat Declan, when they were thirteen, started going to martial arts lessons down the St Padraig's Community Harmony Centre & Cagefighting Club. He wanted to learn how to handle himself in a fight after he was beaten up at school. But he deserved to be beaten up. He was a knob. In fact, he was a brown belt in that. He should have been proud of what he was good at, and taken the consequences.

KIDS' MENUS

They started doing these feckin' everywhere, but I don't know what was wrong with a plate and a spare fork. Any child too small to finish a carvery platter can have the bits of mine that I can't be arsed with. That way the nipper gets a good healthy diet of weird cabbage parts and dark meat to help them grow up big and strong, and I get a nice clean plate. I'm not giving them their own dinky little saucer of chicken nuggets they can leave half of. Waste of feckin' money, that is. And what part of a chicken is the nugget anyway? Is it that dangly bit under the beak? It's feckin' chewy, whatever it's meant to be.

I think it's meant to stop kids kicking off and making a racket where people are eating. You know, give them what they want. But kids don't want cheesy pasta or fish fingers or potato dinosaur shapes. They want sweets. They should put out a feckin' big bowl of Haribo, and some sachets of red sauce, and have done with it.

SHUT THE FECK UP, KIDS!

CHOOSE FROM THE FOLLOWING

CHICKEN NUGGETS

FISH FINGERS

SWEETS

LEFTOVER CABBAGE

SPOT THE DIFFERENCE

ANSWER: THERE IS NONE

PUZZLE TIME

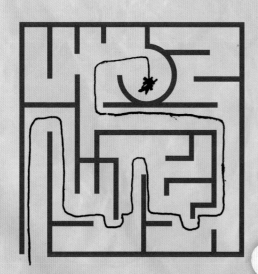

G	I	B	L	E	T
R	A	P	B	D	U
O	E	E	D	I	P
I	E	N	H	L	M
N	S	I	C	D	E
P	M	S	L	O	T

KNITTING

Knitting is an excellent way of making a
tutting sound without moving your lips. You
can criticize an entire room without talking.
And you get a lovely scarf out of it at the end.

IS FOR...

LAUNDRY

Right. This is the bit I was born to write. There is literally nothing I don't know about laundry. Any Mammy worth her salt would say this. And, like a decent packet of chips, I'm worth me salt.

MRS BROWN'S LAUNDRY GUIDE

ALL YOU WILL
EVER NEED TO KNOW

THE INVENTION OF LAUNDRY

Back in the olden days, people lived in mud, slept in holes and spent all day chasing mammoths for fun. I expect. I mean, I'm not exactly an expert on your caveman. There's a limited space in the human brain, and I use a lot for spin cycles.

But I know enough. I've seen Tarzan. The man looks like he hasn't been near a bar of soap since the dawn of time. That's what comes of being raised by monkeys: you end up with no basic grooming skills beyond picking at each other's necks and eating it.

Of course, Tarzan got lucky when he met Jane, and she encouraged him to look after himself a bit better. I expect. I mean, I'm not exactly an expert on Tarzan either.

But he and Jane must have had Little Tarzans and Little Janes, or there wouldn't be a Tarzan family alive today. Which I'm pretty sure there is, because there's one works down the bus station. He even makes that terrible noise when he sneezes.

Now, imagine you're a caveman's wife. The love of your life comes home, knackered after a day throwing spears at woolly elephants, his loincloth absolutely caked in shite. He's got a big day ahead of him tomorrow, because his caveman boss is coming to inspect his hunting, and he wants to look his best. What do you do?

Well, come on now, you're a woman. You're resourceful. You think, 'I know, I'll take his nibs's furry pants down to the stream, give them a good old to and fro in the water, and hang them out on that branch to dry.'

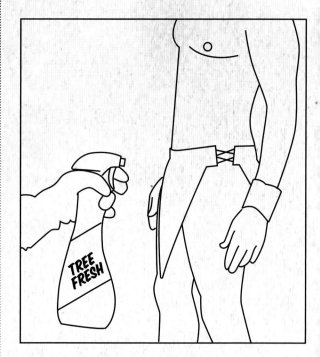

Fig. 1: Survival of the freshest

Bingo. When Mr Caveman gets up the next day, his loincloth's all fresh and he feels like a winner and smells like a tree.

The caveman who smelled the best was going to be the most fanciable, right? Certainly next to some parade of furry buggers who smell worse than a horsebox fire. So the most laundered caveman naturally got the busiest with the biggest number of cavewomen. And he'd naturally choose the ones who were best at laundry, and between them they'd leave the most chisellers behind. Pretty soon the men who didn't like being clean and the women who couldn't give a shite about laundry were bred out of the species, until we reach the peak of womanhood, the perfectly evolved being: a woman who cares about almost *nothing but* laundry. I'm not making any claims, but this is basic science and I don't make the rules.

And that's how laundry was invented. I expect.

ANCIENT EGYPTIAN LAUNDRY

The Ancient Egyptians were a funny bunch, so they were. They had triangular buildings and too much make-up. Very much the fashionizzas of their day. And, let's be honest, their clothes were a bit fancy. You can see it on the films. All gold and orange and blue – lots of shiny stuff that takes a feckin' month to iron. Plus some things that might as well be made out of curtains, they look so bucking heavy.

Of course, because they were a posh lot, the Egyptians had servants. So while all the Cleopatras and Pharaohs (I looked that spelling up, and I still don't think it's right) were upstairs in the pyramid, having their snakes pampered in milk baths, downstairs there was an army of worker Egyptians running the household.

It was exactly like *Upstairs, Downstairs*. I expect. I mean, I'm not exactly an expert on Ancient Egypt.

But I can imagine a whole bevy of beautiful young things all busy scraping away at Elizabeth Taylor's glamorous wardrobe with pumice stones, trying to get the make-up off her cuffs.

According to my researches (Cathy's sitting next to me with her computer), your Ancient Egyptians used the following things for soap:

- **Salt**
- **Lettuce**
- **Swabu**
- **Natron**

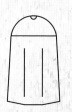

Right.

Well, I'm sure you can all imagine how salt and lettuce would work, and I don't need to tell you what swabu and natron are, do I? (Can somebody check this before the book gets into the shops? I've got a funny feeling I bought some Natron from the chemist's once when Grandad needed unblocking. And I think Father Damien drives a Swabu.)

Also, to keep their clothes extra clean, the men were circumcised. I mean, it makes a sort of sense, but what was it like before then? And who brought it up? No wonder the Sphinx cut its own feckin' nose off. Right, let's move on before this gets unpleasant.

ROMAN LAUNDRY

Oh Jaysus.
I know what's coming.

Once upon a time, Rome was the most important place in the world. A bit like Argos is now. The place was packed with gladiators, grapes and men wearing dresses. (Nothing wrong with that.)

The Ancient Romans (wait for this, you'll love it) had teams of young men standing in bowls of wet laundry with their skirts hitched up, treading it clean. (I know. I know. But there's more.)

Instead of Persil or Omo, they used piss. (Honest – Cathy's just reading this out to me off the Wikipedimajaysewhat.) They collected it in great piss buckets placed on the corner of the street. And when there wasn't enough, they used horse piss. (Feck, me sides. If I laugh any harder, I might be letting a bit of Roman Persil go.)

When the clothes were clean (and I'd like to see what they thought that was), they were hung out to dry, then (here we go again) brushed with hedgehog skins.

Honestly, I had no idea the Romans had such a good sense of humour. I thought it was all stabbing each other with swords and standing around babbling away in capital letters. I've seen

I, Claudius. Well, I've seen two minutes of it on one of the channels in the 400s before I switched over because I was frightened someone was about to marry his horse. I tell you, I watched the whole of Zirconium Heirloom Circlet Afternoon on 952, and when I switched back, they were still going. It goes on even longer than the Roman Empire did, and makes less sense. It's like cricket in bed sheets.

I expect this is why Roman Catholics wanted to be named after the Romans: makes it sound like they're a fun-loving bunch of pisstakers. Well, one out of two's not bad.

Instead of Persil or Omo, they used piss.

THE SAME TRUSTED FORMULA

VIKING LAUNDRY

Now the Vikings were a vicious bunch. And they had the worst possible clothes to wash. I've got a fur or two. Well, one. And I've had it so long I can't remember if it's real or fake or something that started out as a nice coat but has since fluffed up and fallen apart so much that's it turned into a fur. But it needs dry cleaning. And I might not know much about the Vikings, but I'd bet an arm and a leg (Grandad's, not mine) that they didn't have dry cleaners.

So how's your Viking going to get his furs clean? Those things pick up muck like nothing else. Especially if the nippers stroke them after they've picked their noses. (I had to cut that particular bit off me fur coat. I covered the patch with a brooch. There's a tip for you.)

They must have just brushed their furs. And you know what happens when you just brush hair, without cleaning it – it gets all greasy and horrible. And full of dandruff. Now, whether your average Viking didn't mind having a vest covered in dandruff is open to question – history hasn't recorded their opinion. But I've seen Grandad in a vest covered in dandruff and it's not a pretty sight. A blancmange with eczema.

There's no evidence the Vikings did laundry of any sort, in fact. They're known for rape and pillage, not drapes and pillows. And, of course, they had great big boats. And they wore horns. (Horns? Furs? Big moustaches? Natural sailors? I can't be the first to think this, but don't the Vikings seem a bit camp to you? I've met friends of Rory who are more butch. Leaving the women behind to take each other roughly up the fjord. I knew all that wench-ravishing was a cover for something.)

What's this doing in here? I said they didn't have dry cleaners, you feckin' halfwits. Haven't you read a word I've written?

MEDIEVIL LAUNDRY

The Medievils were the second cavemen, except they had huts and no mammoths. But they were all covered in shite, bless them, and their clothes were appalling. Not a lot better than rags. I expect. I mean, I'm not much of an expert on the Medievils.

I know they ate a lot of turnips, though. And lived with their animals, like our Lord in the maternity suite. As far as I can tell from all the pictures, they did feck-all laundry.

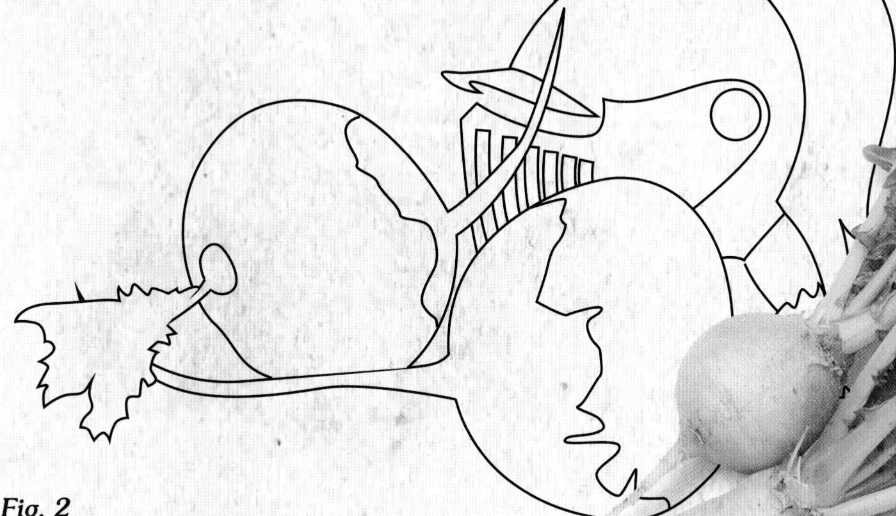

*Fig. 2
Medievil man loved turnips*

18TH-CENTURY LAUNDRY

By the 1700s (which is the 18th century, for some feckin' reason, and don't get me started on that), people had started wearing proper clothes again. Fancy stuff, too: knee-high socks, fancy coats, waistcoats, silly frilly shirts, great big dresses that make the poor lass look like a giant keyhole – and wigs and hats and fans and gloves and canes.

The 18th century must have been bucking freezing, come to think of it. Everyone was wearing about five times as many clothes as they need to. (Bit like you do when you fly Ryanair and only want to take hand luggage – just wear everything you can from your suitcase. My personal best is nine cardigans. I looked like the world's biggest ball of wool.)

But they were a cheeky lot, the 18th Centurians. (Do they have a name? One of the book lot will know.) *They only washed their undies.* Now, I'm not saying this is the way to stay fresh and fragrant – especially not with some of the nice polyester mixes you can get at Boyers – but these poor powdered sods were wearing coats and dresses that were only slightly softer than wood.

So, once a week, all the women in the house would get together and dump everything in great boiling pots and thrash it around with great big paddles. They must have had muscles like Russian shot-putters. When Cathy got that half-price gym membership, it was only a couple of weeks before she looked like feckin' Popeye. I dread to think what would have happened if an 18th-century fella had got his lassie cheesed off about something. One slap and he'd have been flying over the castle roof. Attagirl!

Fig. 3
We only wash our pants...

156

If it was a coloured wash, the ladies might add a magic ingredient: something squeezed out of a cow's gall bladder. Now, I'm not an expert on cow's gall bladders, but I'll bet anything that comes out of them stinks like the back stairs in a Tramp Museum, so you're not talking Pine Fresh or Lemon Sunlight or any of the popular fragrances of today. You're talking Mongol Herdsman's Instep. Not nice.

The best thing about 18th-century wash day was the drying. They used to hang all the clothes over hedges, so it looked like the whole garden was under dust sheets ready for the decorator. Mind you, I don't like the thought of anything sharp snapping off those bushes and becoming lodged in my smalls. There's nothing worse than finding a prick in your pants in the morning. (Which I did whenever Redser was a bit hung over and accidentally went for the wrong drawer while he was getting dressed.)

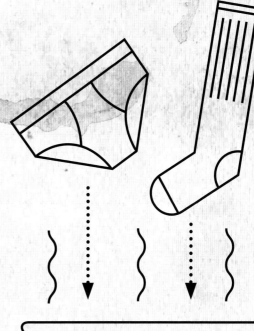

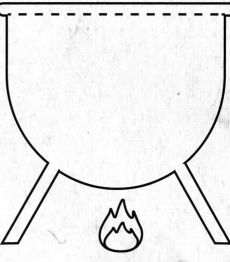

Fig. 4: Essential weekly wash

19TH-CENTURY LAUNDRY

When you read about the Victorians, it's all sooty urchins and workhouses and Jack the Rippers. Sure, wouldn't your Jack the Ripper have had a hell of a time washing the blood off his murderer's overalls? I'd hate to have been his Mammy. All that boil washing. Not to mention the looks from other Mammies whose chisellers haven't chosen a career in ripping.

The Victorians were a filthy lot. If they weren't shoving each other up chimneys, they were up to their ankles in horse shite. And the poor were even worse off. Sometimes there were eleven or twelve of them packed in one tiny room. Like Christmas in my kitchen. Or the confessional when that visiting priest from Brazil was over and the queue stretched almost as far as the feckin' airport. We had to be forgiven in batches, alphabetically. I tell you, it gets hot in those little cupboards when there are more than about five of you fighting for absolution.

Washing day for your Victorian Mammy was a fearsome chore – unless you were Lady Hoity-Toity of Moneytown with an army of poor people to do your smalls for you.

You look at the photos and all the poor Mammies look about 85, even if they're 19.

And it's no wonder. They're worn to a soapy skeleton by a lifetime of hardcore laundry. They had to load all the clothes, wash each bit on its own, starch the collars, lye the whites – it's a wonder they had any hands left by the end of it. Jaysus, even dipping my hands in washing-up liquid leaves them feeling like a pair of concrete gloves. And I've got moisturizer. (Well, cold cream. It's all the feckin' same if you ask me. You're not fooling me by putting a made-up word like Naturollix and a picture of a leaf on a tube of cold cream.)

BUT – and it's a big but, like Hilliary's – the Mammy had something on her side. The mangle.

I remember my Mammy using one of these. I think my Dad had made it for her: half a bicycle smashed round a pair of rolling pins. It might sound like an unending joyless chore, yanking away until your arms ache, but so does helping yourself under the duvet, and plenty of people seem to like doing that.

With the mangle, when Victorian Mammy put her laundry out to dry, it no longer dripped worse than Buster after the police fished him out of the Grand Canal. (He never did get his Tamagotchi back.) And now her laundry was halfway to done, the Victorian Mammy was liberated from laundry

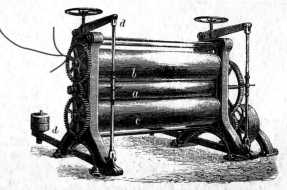

drudgery! At last she was a free woman, able to concentrate on other things, like beating the carpets, cleaning the grates, blacking the stove, laying the fires, filling the oil lamps, scrubbing the step, fetching the water, cooking the supper, cleaning the curtains, dealing with the rent man, and raising about fourteen children in one poky little dust-filled room the size of a feckin' block of butter.

Is it any wonder Whatshername threw herself under that horse? I'd have been ready to throw myself under a herd of feckin' elephants after one day of that. (Makes you wonder were there any Stone Age Suffering Jets who threw themselves under mammoths. I wouldn't have blamed them. Have you tried lighting a fire with two stones? It'd be easier to cut your hair with a spoon.)

When it was all done, Mammy would hang the clothes out, either in the street or indoors, if it was raining. Can't have been much fun to be stuck in a tiny room strung with loads of bed

Fig. 5: Beating the rug
A Victorian lady spent many an hour beating away happily at her rug

sheets and long johns and vests and buck knows what else. Must have been like playing sardines with a load of ghosts.

Anyway, there's a good reason all the Victorian Mammies are dead: exhaustion. Poor cows.

I bet they lay awake every night of their poor lives, resting on their enormous Schwarzenegger arms, every blanket they owned swinging from the rafters, fantasizing about that nice Mr Zanussi coming over from Italy to save them.

Fig. 6: The Victorian lady
Demure face … Schwarzenegger biceps

EARLY 20TH-CENTURY LAUNDRY

The answer was just around the corner for Mammy. The washing machine. She'd saved up her pennies, and was about to buy one, when the First World War came along and put a stop to all that fancy.

Then, after the war, she started popping the pennies in the jar again. And she'd just scraped enough together when along came another feckin' war and Mammy had to put the washing machine on the back burner again. Fair enough, by the time the shop delivered it, the parts would have been repurposed for the war effort and the feckin' thing'd have had a rear gunner.

Typical men. As soon as a Mammy's got something in her sights, along comes a fella with a temper and bollixes it all up. Usually one with a moustache. Never trust a man with a moustache. They're all the same: Hitler, Stalin, Freddie Mercury. Nuts, the lot of them.

Fig. 7: All men with moustaches are nuts

THE WASHING MACHINE

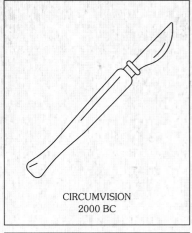

CIRCUMVISION
2000 BC

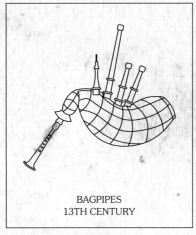

BAGPIPES
13TH CENTURY

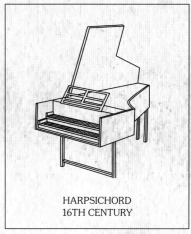

HARPSICHORD
16TH CENTURY

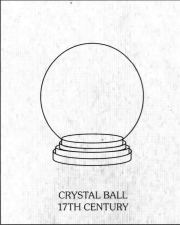

CRYSTAL BALL
17TH CENTURY

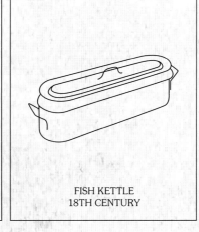

FISH KETTLE
18TH CENTURY

WASHING MACHINE
20TH CENTURY

AT LAST. What took you so feckin' long? It's been 2,000,000 years since that first cavemammy dipped her man's loincloth in the stream. What have you been doing all this time? Dicking about, of course. I mean, how can you (hello, yes, you, men) have invented the *harpsichord* before the washing machine? Did you think you were helping? And what about chess? And crystal balls? And pickled walnuts? And rugby and bagpipes and binoculars and detachable shirt fronts and fish kettles and stained glass and fireworks and guillotines and candy floss and motorbikes and opera and crisps and corsets and ghosts and purple and circumvision? You invented all that shite before the washing machine?

You're all eejits. Thick as two bricks.

THE TUMBLE-DRYER

Do not tumble-dry grandad

Well, at least you gobdaws got the message and didn't hang around another couple of million years before doing something else for Mammy. Pretty quickly after the washing machine got its feet under the counter, along came the tumble-dryer.

Now, I'm a fan of a tumbler meself. There's nothing worse than seeing clothes strung up all round the house like someone put a bomb in your underwear drawer.

But you've not to put everything in a tumbler-dryer. Some things are best left neatly folded up in the hot press. (Like Dermot's grot mags, as I found out while I was looking for the best tablecloth. Jaysus, some of those girls must be double-jointed in places I don't even have one joint.)

Otherwise, your tumble-dryer is your second-best friend. Some people like to do their towels on the line, but they finish up like giant scouring pads if there's not enough breeze. Good if you want to get the flakes off Grandad, but horrible if you're looking to wrap yourself in something soft and warm after a long, hot soak. (I'm talking about a bath, by the way, before you get any modern ideas.)

THINGS NOT TO PUT IN THE TUMBLE-DRYER INCLUDE:

🐑	Wool (because it turns into tiny wool that scratches the bejaysus out of you)
🐛	Silk (because it turns into screwed-up Bible paper)
🐕	Dogs (because they panic, and you know what happens when a dog panics)
🦯	Grandad (because all that motion brings out the beast in him)
🌿	Salad (because it doesn't dry properly and some of the tomatoes burst)
🍽️	Washing-up (pay attention, Buster, it's not a feckin' dishwasher, you gommo)

THOSE LITTLE SYMBOLS

They say every Mammy needs to know what those tiny scribbles on clothes labels mean. I say away and take your bollix with you.

All that feckin' fiddly nonsense is for scientists and people who read the small print on packets of nuts in case they contain nuts. All as you need to know is: colours low, whites high, softies cold. That's it. You can get wristbands with it on, if you're forgetful.

Colours low, whites high, softies cold.

I find it helps to sing it to the tune of 'Amazing Grace'. (I had this done with the dots by Martin who plays the Bontempi at the seamen's mission.)

Amazing Grace

A – maz-ing— way to do your clothes:

Co–lours low, whites high, soft-ies cold

THOSE LITTLE SYMBOLS (continued)

If you've stared at the label on the collar of a 20-per-cent-polyester sports top, wondering if you're about to wash it into an Action Man jerkin, you'll be after knowing what those baffling hierobloodyglyphics mean.

Here's Mammy's guide.

30°	You're only as old as the men you fancy.
95°	Although this is how old you look first thing in the morning.
△	It's never too early for a Toblerone.
(triangle crossed out)	And now you've eaten the whole feckin' thing.
(tub)	Finish the washing-up first.
(hand in tub)	Now wash your filthy feckin' hands.
P	Grandad's trousers. Handle with care.
W	What the fuck has he been eating?
F	Forget it. You'll never get that stain out.
(crossed out)	This is no time for a gin and orange. Not even a little one.

INSTRUCTIONS
Wash your feckin' hands.
Have a Toblerone.
Have a nice cup of tea.
Have yourself a lie down.

○	Have a cup of tea instead.
▥	And one of those nice biscuits.
△	Would you look at that? Someone's left a road cone in the hedge again.
○	Mind you, sun's out. Maybe I might have that gin after all.
⊗̸	GRANDAD! WHERE'S ALL MY FECKIN' GIN GONE?
Ⓐ	Arsehole.
○	I'll have another cup of tea.
▨	And maybe just a little slice of cake. Terrible sweet tooth, me.
⊔•	Ah, bollix. I'll have an advocaat. With a little cherry in it.
✍	Mammy's little helper. Advocaat.

⊔••	Might have another. And an extra cherry.
⊔—	Feel a bit wobbly now.
✕	What was I doing again?
▢○	The laundry. That was it. Right. Washing machine.
▢⊗̸	No. That's not the washing machine.
▣●	Right so. There it is.
70°	Might as well put it on motorway setting. Get it over quicker.
▢••	Jaysus, Agnes. Look at yourself. Either your mirror's not working or you're half cut.
⋈̸	Don't start on the chocolates. That won't help.
▽	Tell you what. I'll just have meself a little lie down.

165

LAUNDRY DOS AND DON'TS

DON'T put Dermot's trainers in the washing machine until you've checked them for frogs.

DO make sure your washing machine is clean inside by doing some feckin' laundry every now and then.
(I'm looking at you, Dirty Deirdre Donovan.)

DON'T use stain remover on anything other than stains. It doesn't get rude words off teenagers' t-shirts, orange and brown patterns off second-hand curtains, or liver spots off Grandad's hands.

DO use softener, even when the instructions tell you not to. The scent of spring blossom covers up the smell of the washing-machine motor getting on a bit.

DON'T put your potatoes in with the boil wash, however much time you think it'll save you. You try getting mash out of the little holes in the drum. It's like trying to pick 800 noses with a soup ladle.

DO get your washing machine serviced at least once a year by Brian O'Noolan of MachineRite Repairs, Lovelyne Road, Dublin. His competitive prices and first-class customer service are absolutely worth the €50 he paid me to write this.

DON'T do your ironing in the garden, even on the nicest day. Nothing can get burned, squashed butterfly off an iron. Not even a chisel.

DO make sure your washing machine is on a level bit of floor, otherwise you might find it leaving the kitchen during the spin cycle and creeping up on Grandad. Then you'll have another load of laundry to do straight away.

DON'T invite me round your house for a spurious feckin' reason, only for me to find out you want to show off to me about your new all-singing, all-dancing, robot washing machine covered in blue lights that has 600 different settings and probably does the ironing afterwards too, Hilliary. We both know you'll never touch the thing, and it'll be that poor woman who cleans for you who has to work out how to programme the onboard feckin' computer.

DO shut up about your new washing machine, Hilliary.

THE ETERNAL MYSTERY OF SOCKS

You buy them in pairs. You put them on in pairs. You take them off in pairs. You put them in the laundry in pairs. And when you get them out of the washing machine, there's one missing.

There's a lot of theories about where the socks go. Some of them are plain feckin' daft. 'The washing machine eats them.' 'They get abducted by aliens.' That sort of bollix.

Now, I've spent a long time thinking about this, and there's only two answers that are possible.

1. They dissolve.

2. They're like rice, and they expand when they get wet – so what goes in as a sock comes out as a spare t-shirt.

Applying science, I have to say I've never found a spare t-shirt (or a spare anything, except some spare change) in my washing machine, so I'm saying they definitely dissolve.

But, wait a minute, you're thinking, 'Mammy – why would sockmakers make some socks that dissolve and others that don't?' Well, I'll tell you. It's because they get bad batches of wool. Remember when they found all that horse meat in minced beef? It's like that all over again. Some of the cheap wool is laced with candy floss by unscrupulous shepherds.

Now there. Haven't you learned something today? I'm telling you, there are cheapskates everywhere. Not just raking through the Past-Their-Sell-By-Date bin at Puntstretcher for a bag of chocolate buttons that have gone a bit corky.

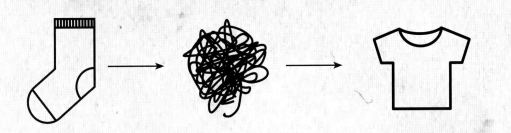

DRY CLEANING

Have you ever wondered to yourself, 'Sure now, why can't I buy a dry-cleaning machine for the home?'

Well, the answer's easy: because they're feckin' huge. They're giant washing machines. They don't run on water, because they're dry, and there's no such thing as dry water, only dry martini, and it'd cost a feckin' fortune to fill one of these machines with martini, and the olives would get smashed all over your frock. So that's a non-starter. Although I don't have a clue what they do run on. Special air or magic or something. It's obviously a secret, like how your man made the Statue of Liberty disappear.

The best thing about the dry cleaner's is the free hangers you get. Mark used to get through dozens of them when the aerial fell off his car. And people were always nicking them. I must have had that sock dry-cleaned 50 times just so he could listen to that Ryan Tumbledry on the radio.

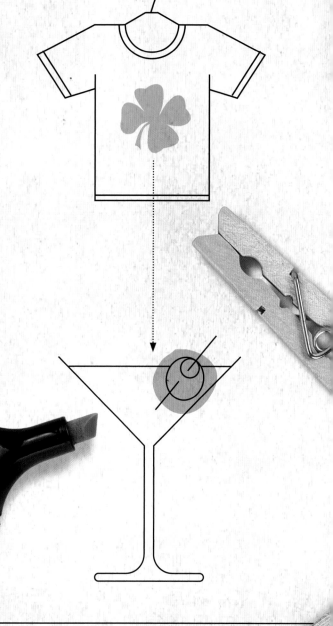

LEGO INJURIES

More accidents happen in the home than anywhere else. I read that when I was in hospital. (Forgot to put any water in the egg-poaching pan. Burned meself on the handle. Fool.)

The kitchen is where most things go wrong. Mammy Hawkins was notorious for her pease pudding volcano. She was never much use in the kitchen. Asked her Molly how she cooked pease pudding. 'Easy,' said Molly, 'put the pease pudding in a saucepan and heat it on the hob.' So Mammy Hawkins put the tin of pease pudding in the saucepan. Didn't open the tin. Molly said she was still finding bits of dried food in the curtain rails ten years later.

But the real bastard around the home isn't in the kitchen: it's everywhere feckin' else. Lego. The kiddies love it (and some of the men do too) and it's meant to be fun, but Jaysus, you try keeping a smile on your face when you tread on it.

Tread on Lego and you can be hopping round the room for a good quarter of an hour. And it can pierce a hole in some of the cheaper hoover bags. Those bricks are lethal. Like little cluster bombs. It would help if they were one colour, but they're loads, so you can't even get a Lego-proof carpet they show up on.

There are really only two ways to avoid Lego injuries:

• Always wear your carpet slippers – and who does? Sure, you can't sleep in them.

• Ban Lego from the house.

• Sell the kids for medical experiments, toys down Barnardo's.

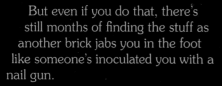

But even if you do that, there's still months of finding the stuff as another brick jabs you in the foot like someone's inoculated you with a nail gun.

Anyway, it's for the kiddies, isn't it? You buy them these toys because you love them. To show them they deserve a treat for all the love they give you back. And to keep them quiet while you watch the Bargain Network.

You'd think science would have invented a Lego detector by now, wouldn't you? I mean, they've got metal detectors so all those weirdos in rain jackets can go wandering round fields finding old cutlery – but yet again, nothing useful for the busy Mammy. There's too many men in science. Science needs a few feckin' women giving the orders.

Mammy's trick, though, was much smarter than that: Lego-absorbing foot protectors. These are dead easy to make, and they work like magic.

You will need:
• a loaf of thickly sliced bread
• Sellotape
• a room where some Lego might be hiding

Here's what you do:

• Take a thick slice of bread and Sellotape it to the sole of your foot.

• Repeat for the other foot.

• Carefully walk around the room where the Lego might be hiding, in straight lines, back and forth, making sure you cover every square inch of carpet you can see.

• At the end of each line, sit down and examine the underneath of your feet. If there was Lego to be found, it'll now be stuck in your bread.

Brilliant, simple and it probably counts as exercise. You might need to change your bread a few times, because it does go pretty flat after a while. And don't forget to hoover up all the crumbs afterwards, otherwise the mice'll think someone's invited them to one of those parties where they have free food. But you will never suffer from Lego injuries again. And that means you can keep the kids.

LIBRARIES

I couldn't have written this book without my local library and an enormous pull-along shopper's trolley.

Some of those books you're not meant to take out of the Reference Library weigh a feckin' ton. The best way to take out a book you're not meant to take out is to get Buster to start a fight in the motor repairs section by refusing to believe they don't have a Haynes Manual for his Batmobile. That takes out most of the sprightlier staff, and the remainder can be occupied stopping Dermot photocopying his arse. When the magnetic alarm's going off, you can wave your hands and point at your side and mouth 'new hip' until the old dear with the glasses on a chain lets you through. Then leg it. And that's how to use the library.

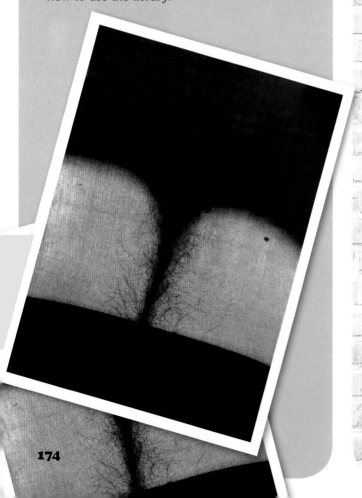

LOFTS

Since mankind has existed, he (or she – I'm not the best to tell the difference) has needed a loft. You can bet your caveman had a loft, up there in the top of his cave, full of Christmas decorations and old cave paintings of his kids when they were younger, and old copies of *The Caveman* that might be worth something someday, and bones his cavegrandfather handed down to him.

Lofts are like half-bins. They're full of stuff you *really must* throw away but *really can't*. It's like getting into the back of the dustcart and waving nicely at the dustmen before they bring the big thing crunching down on everything you've chucked away.

I've seen this somewhere else. Now where have I seen this?

I KNOW WHERE!

On Cathy's computer. That's where. She has a thing called 'Trash', which is shaped like a wastepaper basket. She throws stuff away, but it just sits there. *Just sits there*, like the poisoned stuff it is. It isn't gone until she empties the trash. I know because I asked her to throw away a picture of me she'd taken that made me look like I had a double chin and skin like a jellyfish – some problem with the camera – and when I clicked on the little picture of the bin, it popped back up in my face like a fat ghost. It hadn't really gone.

That's what your loft is. It's stuff you've thrown away, but haven't. It's the bin, before you've emptied it. It's the halfway point between 'rubbish' and 'gone for ever'. It's a museum of crap. That's what it is: a Museum of Crap.

THE CAVEMAN

BEST SAUSAGES TO FEED YOUR MAN

10 BONES

THE MUSEUM OF CRAP

PARTS

So every house has its little Museum of Crap. Mine has some glorious exhibits: old games and toys and jigsaws with bits missing, baby stuff (which I can only assume I've kept just in case I get pregnant again at the age of 85), VHS tapes of stuff I'm never going to watch again, the VHS machine I'd need to watch it on, boxes of stuff the kids have put up there (diaries, in Cathy's case; grot mags, in the boys' case – I'm guessing. I'm just guessing. I haven't seen Lydia, aged 23, from Romford, with her 'considerable assets' and her 'big future in front of her' and her 'arse'. And nor have you, if anyone asks.)

Every piece of crap has a memory attached though, which is why it's so hard to throw it away. It goes up into the hole, ascending into crap heaven, and it never comes down. You're holding on to the past, because you know, in your heart, it's leaving you, one child at a time. It's sentiment, I suppose. That and not wanting to risk going up that ladder Redser put in, the one with the step that drops when you put your weight on it and threatens to slice the toes off your feckin' slippers.

There's weird stuff up there too that fair staggers the imagination. Rolls of loft insulation, but balanced on top of old paint cans. A bin bag of assorted parts for something – no idea what – labelled 'PARTS' in Tippex. Some feckin' terrifying piece of exercise equipment that looks like something out of a torture chamber, that's been used once and hidden. A bottle of something marked 'NOT WINE'. (It might be 'NOT MINE' – the handwriting's a bit shaky.) One of them blind-girl charity boxes that used to be chained up outside the shops. (I think Redser might have had designs on using it as a statue. It's still full of coins, but nothing legal tender.) A book on how to convert your loft. (Ah, forgotten ambitions.) An artificial leg. (No idea. One of Dermot's pranks?) And the centrepiece of it all: the old cold-water tank. When it went wrong and sprang a leak, Mark put a new one in, but the old one was too big to get out of the hatch so it's up there still, except now it's full of shoes and Lego instead of water and dead birds.

If you've got a cellar and a loft, your house is basically a crap sandwich.

Prosthetic leg
Mixed media

Not wine/mine?
Unknown media

LOVE

Love is a mystery. Not the normal sort of mystery where everyone gets together in a room at the end and the detective explains who did it and one of them tries to climb out the window, but a more mysterious sort of mystery.

What is it that makes someone want to stay with somebody else for years and years? Not a custodial sentence but that tugging in the heart that makes it unthinkable to spend your lives apart? You're in each other's hair, you're driving each other berserk…but if you're going to throw pans at someone, *they're* the one you want to throw pans at.

That's a special sort of madness, like believing you're Napoleon or that you may already have won a big prize in this draw. Proper madness. And it's beautiful.

They say opposites attract, that the best couples are ones where you each have a different thing to bring to the table. In my case it was dinner. Every night. For Redser. Like clockwork. I may not have known much about the mysteries of love, shy newlywed slip of a girl as I was, but I knew the way to a man's heart. Sausages. As this illustration clearly shows:

Look at it. That's the human heart. And what's that you can see wrapped round it on every side? Sausages.

Blue and red ones, for some reason. I imagine the fella who drew it was taking a bit of the old autistic licence, or some herbal cigarettes like Dermot got in trouble for at scouts, but the human heart is wrapped in sausages. No idea why, I'm no doctor, but it definitely proves my point.

I

You

Love is about providing for each other. Whether it's providing food for the stomach or comfort for the soul. It's making someone as important in your life as you are, if not more. A proper lover puts you in front of them, will bend over backwards and cover your back. I know, I've seen it. Winnie found a book in Jacko's sock drawer with pictures you wouldn't believe.

And then there's that other sort of love. The love a Mammy has for her children. The love a man has for his lawnmower. The love a brother has for his sister. Maybe it's deeper. You'd certainly hope it's less sexual. Especially with the lawnmower. A man could end up suffering crippling cuts to his family allowance after a fling with a Qualcast.

The strongest love of all is a Mammy's love. It can move mountains. You'd lift a car off a kiddie, especially if it was you who parked it there in the first place. It's an animal love, like the lion protecting her cubs or the silverback ant protecting her caterpillars (note: check this in insect fact book when Mark gets out of the toilet).

Love is so many things: love is patient, love is kind, love is never having to say sorry, love gives great results even at low temperatures. That last one might not be about love, actually; I'm copying these off the fridge magnets.

Look at my family. There's proof, if ever you needed it, that there's no rules for love. It comes in all shapes and sizes. But without it, you're lost.

And however you love, do remember to wash your hands afterwards.

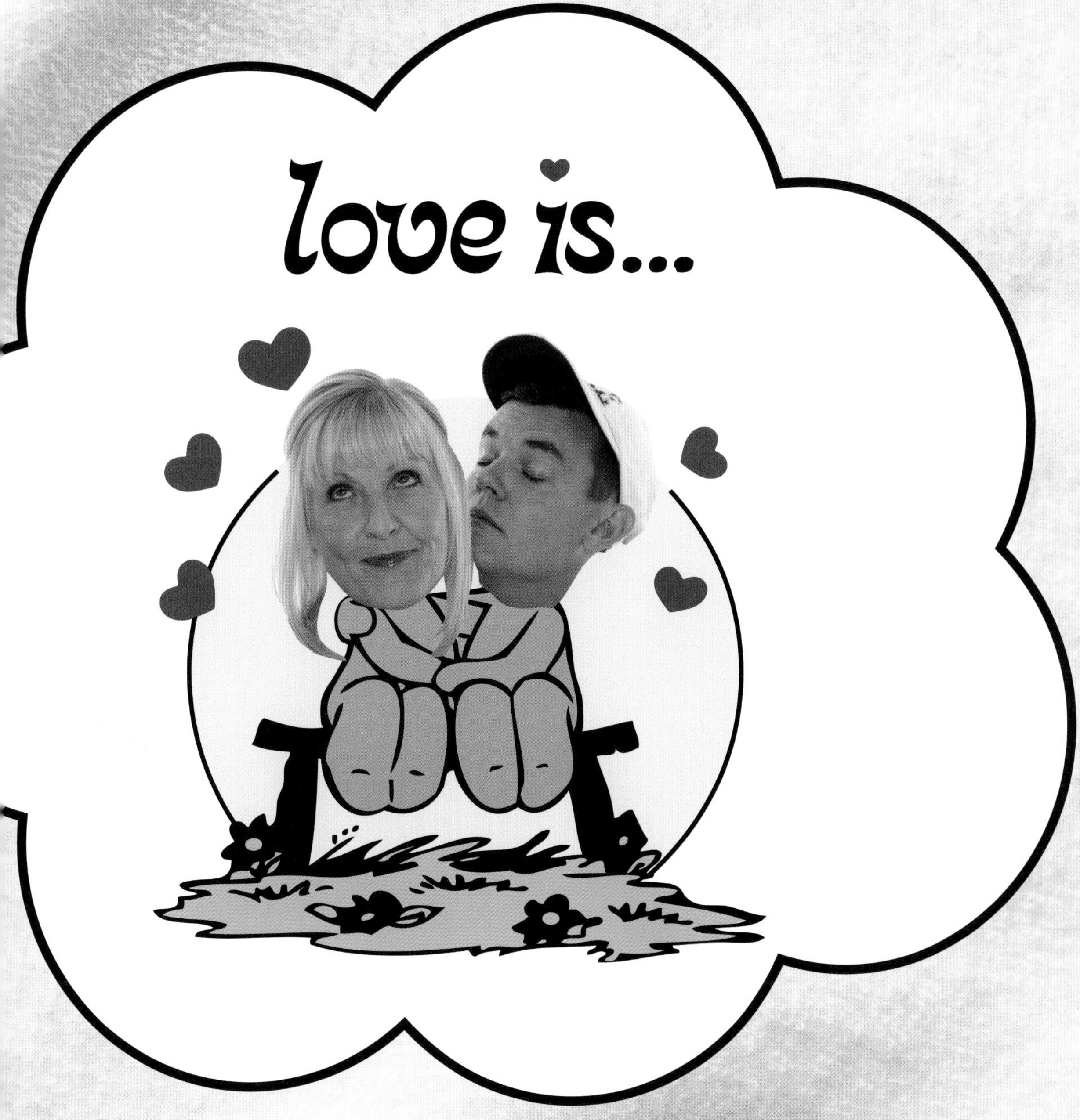
love is...

IS FOR...
MIRRORS

MAGNETISM,
MAN ON THE MOON,
MAP READING,
MARGRINE,
MATTER,
MONEY,
MONSTERS,
MOTHER'S DAY,
MOTHS,
MOUSTACHES

M IS FOR... MIRRORS

MAGNETISM,
MAN ON THE MOON,
MAP READING,
MARCHING!
MATTER,
MONEY,
MONSTERS,
MOTHER'S DAY,
MOTHS,
MOUSTACHES

etism

is the word for how a black piece of metal is naturally attracted to a white piece of metal and that's how fridge magnets work

No he feckin' didn't. I saw one of those 'how it's done' programmes on the telly, a documentally, in one of the high-numbered channels near the shops, and they explained pretty damn clearly how it wasn't done.

Apparently, they faked the whole thing up in Hollywood because it's impossible to go to the moon. That makes perfect sense to me. That's their usual way with this sort of thing, the space sort of thing, as I understand it: it's not real and it only happens in films.

So what they expect us to swallow is that, right, *all* the other space things, they're only in films. But this *one* space thing – the going to the moon one – that one's real?

The one from ages ago, before we even had microwave feckin' ovens, that one's real? Pull the other one. I know how it works, when they can't find an actual Star War to film, they just fake it up, with robots and midgets dressed up.

Here's how it's done, as far as I can gather. They get your Buzz Lightyear and your Louis Armstrong, they put them in the spacesuits, in the rocket. Let them wave to the crowd. Then they drive the rocket to Hollywood, and they put them in a film studio where they're already filming a moon thing, so they've got the craters. They tell Captain Spock to go and get himself some soup and a buttered roll, and while nobody's looking they film the whole thing, all the bouncing and that, and the flag, and they nip off before anyone notices and Bob's your uncle: it looks like they landed on the moon. What could be simpler?

Mark says we definitely did land on the moon, and that if scientists weren't able to put a rocket into space, we wouldn't have satellites, and that would mean the computerized where-to-go-doohicky in his car wouldn't work and neither would his phone, but whenever I call his Betty to have a stiff word about something important, she says the signal's breaking up and she has to go, so that's *that* answered.

Plus Mark wouldn't go to sleep one night until I'd checked under the bed in case there were Daleks, so I'm not trusting his judgement on matters galactic.

Louis Armstrong
the first man
on the moon

READING A MAP IS IMPOSSIBLE

LET'S GET THIS STRAIGHT: IT IS *IMPOSSIBLE* TO READ A MAP. I KNOW PEOPLE WHO SAY THEY CAN, BUT IT CAN'T BE DONE. IT'D BE EASIER TO FECKIN' *EAT* A MAP THAN READ ONE.

Men pretend they can read maps, but they can't really. They pretend to because

- it stops them having to talk to someone and ask directions, and

- it stops them having to talk to you.

They can hide behind a map, umm-ing and ah-ing and pretending they know what in feck's name all the little squiggles mean, but it's the same as hiding behind a newspaper –

IT'S NOT A MAP, IT'S A WALL.

MAP READING

You can tell they're not really reading the map, because they don't turn it round all different ways, which is how you read a map. Give a map to a woman, she turns it round, so she can imagine herself standing in the map. 'If I'm here, then that's forwards, and that's left…Oh bollix. We're lost.' And then she asks directions. A man just stares at it, making little noises. I think they just like the colours.

Maybe maps are like those Magic Eye pictures they had a while back. I never saw bollix all in them either. If you want to see something interesting in a load of rubbish, come and have a sort through my bins. There's usually a *Woman's Way* in there with a story about someone who got so fat they had to be taken to hospital on a bulldozer.

Mark says he can read a map, but he's got one of those automatic computer SatNags in the car, you know, those robot women that nag you to go left and all that. And that's yet another perfectly good job lost to robotification.

Still, he tried to teach me to read a map once, and he drew me a sort of quiz to test how much I'd taken in. This is what I put, and he never asked me again, so I assume I got them all right.

So if you did want to try and learn to read a map, which is impossible, you could do worse than start here and learn from me.

Symbols on a Standard 1:25,000 Map

1

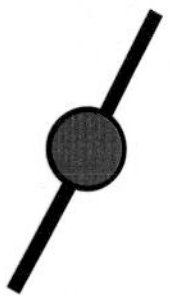

Cocktail bar

2

Vasectomy clinic

3

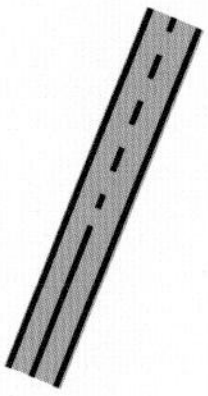

Jeans shop

4

Strawberry
bootlaces

5

Good place for
a pee

6

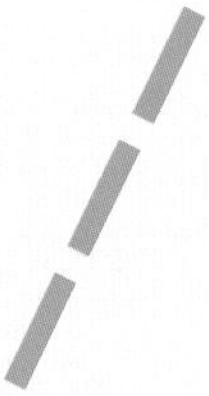

Good place for
an urgent pee

7

Two of diamonds

8

Red Indians
on holiday

9

Teddy bear's nose

Symbols on a Standard 1:25,000 Map

10

Haunted ball? No idea

11

Hilliary's feckin' silly house

12

McDonald's

13

Ann Stunners shop

14

Boring day out

15

Lemon drizzle cake

16

Dermot at work

17

Biscuits

18

Funeral director's

Symbols on a Standard 1:25,000 Map

19

Eye tests available

20

Haunted box

21

Mickey Mouse club

22

Toilet

23

Family of mice
attracted by crumbs

24

Hula-hooping contest

25

DANGER!
Landmines

26

Little fella
on spacehopper

27

Little fella in
a go-kart

Symbols on a Standard 1:25,000 Map

28

$+$

Little fella buried
in the sand

29

Entertainment
question

30

Sch

Be quiet!

31

PO

Piss off!

32

PC

Police station

33

Strawberry creme

34

Doctor's
handwriting

35

One of them optical illusions
where they're both the same size

36

Video arcade

195

Symbols on a Standard 1:25,000 Map

37
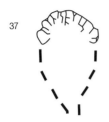

Mick Hucknall

38

FB

Feckin' bus

39

∘W
∘Spr

Wonder Woman/
Superman

40

WARNING:
men farting everywhere

41

WARNING:
men pissing everywhere

42

Teenagers'
moustaches

43

Six of clubs

44

Old ladies' moustaches

45

Nice long bath

Symbols on a Standard 1:25,000 Map

46

Varicose veins

47

Champagne bar

48

Lentil soup

49

Mushroom soup

MARGARINE

Filth. Won't have it in the house. Tastes like plastic, looks like plastic. Like some plastic dairymaid has made it out of the plastic milk she yanked out the plastic tits of a plastic cow.

BUTTER

MARGARINE

MATTER

Matter, so the boffins say, when they aren't busy writing gibberish all over blackboards, is what the whole universe is made of. Everything is made of matter. That's where we get the phrase 'What's the matter?' Because there's always something the matter. You know how it is.

There are four flavours of matter.

1. Solids
2. Liquids
3. Gas
4. Stuff that doesn't matter

1. Solids

Solids are the basics – marriage, kids, food, the roof over your head, TV, a kind word, sausages, coupons, clothes (see Laundry), having a laugh, scraping by, telling the truth, cleaning the oven, popping your spare change in a charity tin, putting up with Grandad – the bread and butter of life.

2. Liquids

Liquids include cider.

3. Gas

Gas is *essential* for cooking, because an electric hob is more difficult to control than a rat on skates. Everything's either not hot enough or it's sticking to the pan. That's why you need gas. Try doing an omelette on an electric hob. One side's the consistency of a runny nose, the other's dark brown and tastes like a mouthful of matches.

If you could cook with electric, you'd be able to do chipolatas in the plug sockets, and I tell you, I've come back fluthered from too much liquid at Foley's, when the kitchen surfaces have seemed a bit too high up, and tried to make a sausage supper in the plug sockets and it's a fool's errand. Well, technically, it's a fireman's errand, but it's a waste of time anyway.

4. Stuff that doesn't matter

Everything else is stuff that doesn't matter: money, yoga, pandas (see Pandas), posh crisps, politics, foot spas, Hilliary (see That Woman), *Star Wars*, bean sprouts (see Weird Vegetables), opera, junk mail, air conditioning, socks that look like gloves, TV cabinets, mouthwash, anything that calls itself a 'tidy', part-time policemen, soups with silly names like 'chowder' and 'skink', water filters, carpet protectors, chopsticks, free samples, revolving doors, knife sharpeners (they're all feckin' useless), chocolate with anything from your main course in it, cling film that's so thin you could breathe a hole in it, umbrella bags, men with long hair, price comparison adverts, wet rooms (ugh), serving suggestions, circuses, cheese with bits in, religions that aren't billions of years old, tiny bananas, hanging baskets, cats, hooped earrings, people in bright-yellow jackets who can't tell you fuck all when you ask them a question, running if you're not being chased, herbal remedies, snakes, quiche, Harry Potter, fire drills, cupcakes, intimate wipes, barbecued vegetables (using up valuable sausage space), gymnastics, retirement homes, midges, rechargeable batteries, sailors' uniforms (they give you the wrong idea), weird jams, posh taxis, carpets that don't reach the walls, birthday cards without badges on them, anything solar powered, anyone who says peanuts aren't nuts, and anything beginning with Z (see Z).

None of it matters.

Get that straight, and you're on the road to understanding the universe.

201

**Who's the fairest
of them all?** ....
This mirror
never lies

MIRRORS

What do you see when you look in the mirror? A buxom, beautiful, distinguished, mature, stylish, refined, easy-going, much-loved, warm-hearted woman of the world? Me too. Although first thing, and before I've got my glasses on, it can look like a fella in drag.

Some people see terrible things: fat versions of themselves, short-arsed versions of themselves. That's why you should never do your make-up in a fairground. Those mirrors are meant to make you look daft. And come on, don't take the piss: if you can afford a night out on the waltzers, stuffing your face with candy floss, you can afford a feckin' bathroom cabinet.

In the really olden days, back when there were cavemen and Vikings and when Jesus himself walked the earth, they didn't have mirrors. They hadn't been invented. You can sort of tell that, because cavemen and Vikings and Jesus all had untidy long hair and great messy beards, and if they'd seen the state of themselves, they'd have gone and got a proper haircut and a wet shave. That's why you never see a bumper sticker: Jesus Shaves. Because he didn't. It's no wonder people were suspicious of him.

But how do mirrors work?
Well, Winnie explained this to me, and it's dead interesting.

***'Winnie's Mirror Theory'* >**

WINNIE'S MIRROR THEORY

Mirrors are basically windows that have been turned off, so you can't see what's behind them, and all you can see is the reflection. (Just a minute. Why doesn't the TV turn into a mirror when you switch it off? Why does it just go all dark? Might have to ask Winnie that.)

And everything in the mirror is the wrong way round. So you're back to front. If you wave with your right hand, your reflection waves back with its left hand, which is where your right hand has ended up. (Just a minute. So why aren't you upside down as well? What's so special about left and right? What have they got that up and down haven't?)

And here's the other thing Winnie told me: if you get into one of those lifts in the hoity-toity department stores that have got mirrors on all four sides, and you look into one of them and there's hundreds of you, getting smaller and smaller off into the distance like you're in a never-ending tunnel of you, vanishing off towards the end of the universe – what you're looking at there is *The Crystal Mind of God.*

I'll tell you what. I'm not 100 per cent sure Winnie's got a feckin' clue what she's on about here. I am about 90 per cent sure she was about 40 per cent proof when she thought all this up. She came back from the toilets in Foley's feckin' convinced, but they've changed the disinfectant in there and it brings up quite a vapour. The Crystal Mind of God. I ask you.

Listen: the practical things you need to know about mirrors are:

(1) Keep them clean, or you might end up trying to squeeze a spot that turns out to be a smutty mark on the glass.

(2) Carry a little one in your purse at all times, because it's dead useful for seeing round the back of the fruit machines with and there's usually some change to be found down there.

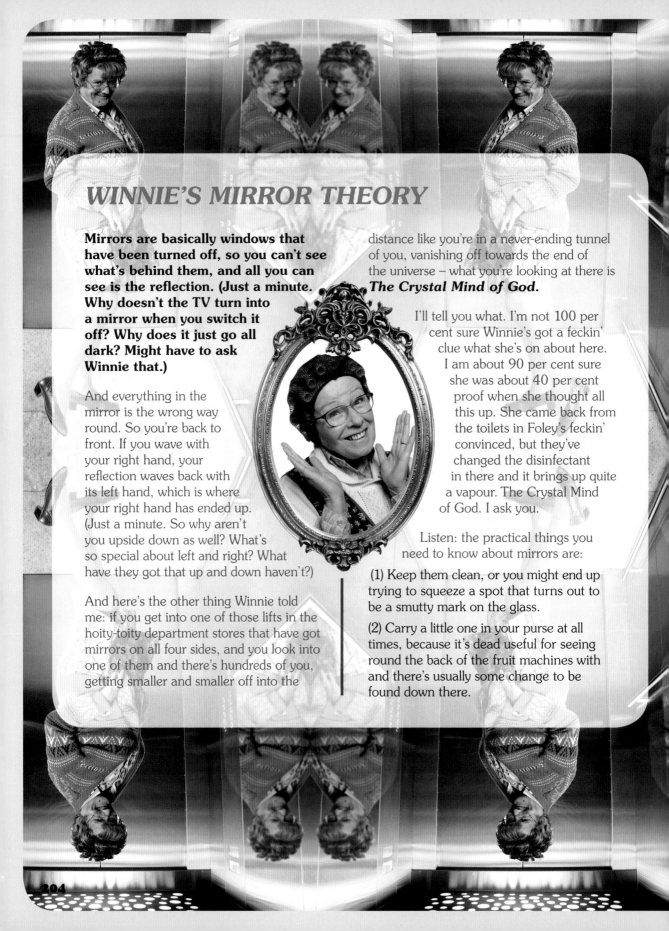

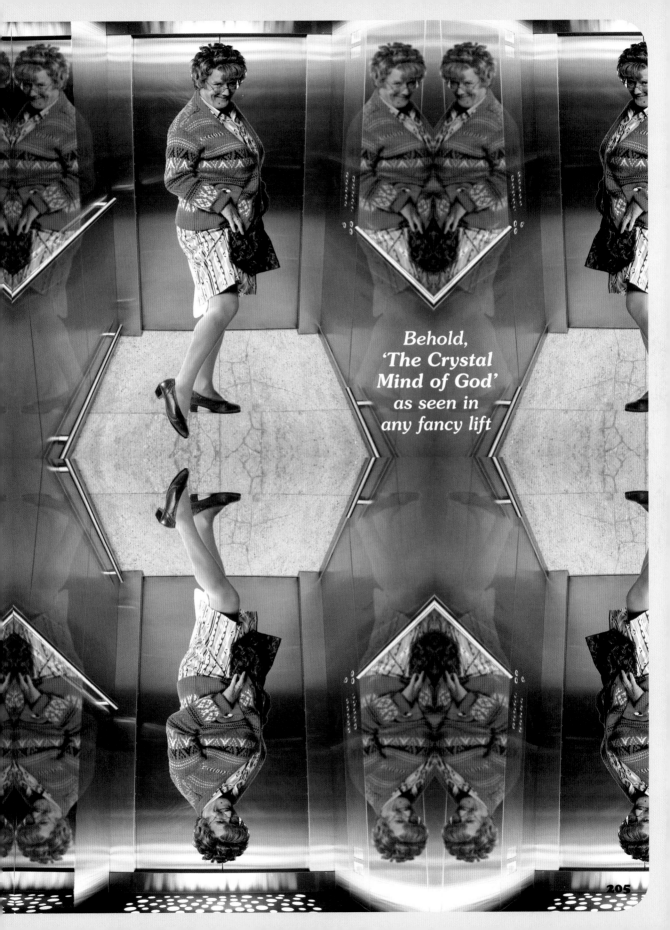

Behold,
'The Crystal
Mind of God'
as seen in
any fancy lift

MONEY

Friends get you by in times of no money better than money in a time with no friends.

My best friend Winnie bought me that on a souvenir plate. But I sold it when I had no money, and the touchy cow didn't talk to me for weeks, so that's that experiment bollixed. They say money can't buy you happiness, but it can put a down payment on not caring.

Friends get you by in times of no money ~

~ better than money in a time with no friends

NEW!
50p

MONSTERS

Forget stuff people have just made up to scare each other, like the Loch Ness Monster and Bigfoot and Zebras – the only real monsters anyone has to worry about are the eight-legged ones.

FECK!

I'm talking about spiders. Spiders are everywhere, because their natural predator, the glass, only evolved recently. They tend to live underneath or above anywhere you're happy (the bath, bed, shed). People say you shouldn't kill spiders because they eat flies, but as long as you kill both spiders and flies, that's not a problem. One place you never see spiders is crawling across your TV, which is a good reason never to turn it off.

MOTHER'S DAY

Father's Day was made up by the greetings card companies and can feck right off.

But Mother's Day is a wonderful chance to show your Mammy how much you love her with a lie-in, a bacon sandwich and a box of chocolates the size of a dustbin lid. It was made up by the card companies as well, but like I give a shite. Don't buy a card. That'll show 'em. As long as I get the sandwich and the lie-in, I'll consider that issue well and truly dealt with.

...No, you really shouldn't have. This is what Mammy really wants for Mother's Day.

MOTHS

Moths are like the evil butterflies that come out when it gets dark. Butterflies are all rainbow colours and flowers and hope. Moths are the up-all-night mopy teenagers, musty as a nun's knicker drawer, and dressed down like undertakers. They're the yobs. The night shift. The skeleton crew. Bastards.

There are two types:

1. The big horrors who flap down out of the porch light like a kamikaze coming out of the sun to frighten the bejaysus out of you when you're putting the milk bottles out last thing.

2. The little bastards who eat your best coat – that one you got for your son's wedding, which you never really liked but it cost a feckin' fortune. (It's not the principle. It's the money.) Idiots. Fancy eating clothes. You'll be telling me they wear food next. What are they? The insect Lady Gaga?

God knows how moths get in wardrobes. Nobody puts them there. They're like coat hangers, and don't get me started on where the feck they come from. And even if you've got your best jacket Sellotaped up airtight in one of those bags you get from the dry cleaner's, the little bastards will still get in there and make a three-course breakfast of your tweed. How do they get in? They're like evil Houdinis.

Whatsisface on the telly says it's not the moths that eat your clothes, it's their littluns, which are worms. That's even more disgusting than having a miserable butterfly in your wardrobe. Worms?

Moths are to butterflies what wasps are to bees (see Wasps). An extra version nobody asked for. They're surplus to requirements, like him out of The Corrs. They're just there to make the other ones look more beautiful. They're annoying and they get in your way. Give them a clipboard and a hi-vis jacket, they could stand on Grafton Street, collaring you for a direct debit for Cystic Fibrosis. That bad.

Fig. 1
Insectus Lady Gaga

Fig. 2
Mopius Teenagerus

Fig. 3
Evillus Butterflyus

Fig. 4
Musty Nun's Underpantus

Fig. 5
Evillus Houdini

Fig. 6
Likeus Lightbulbus

Fig. 7
Likeus Clothesus

Don't believe any of that namby-pamby rubbish about having cedarwood in your wardrobe or lavender bags or sprinkling pepper on your best cardie. (Like you want a feckin' attack of the sneezes when you're under siege.) The only way to get rid of moths is to get the council in. Moths are allergic to the council or something. (And if they send their man round with the chemical spray, get them to give Grandad the once over, just in case. I've no idea what little forms of life he's incubating in that thermal underwear of his, but I bet they're not the nice ones they hide in yoghurt.)

Other things moths like to eat:

- Carpets.
- Curtains.
- Crisps, probably.
  Everyone likes crisps.

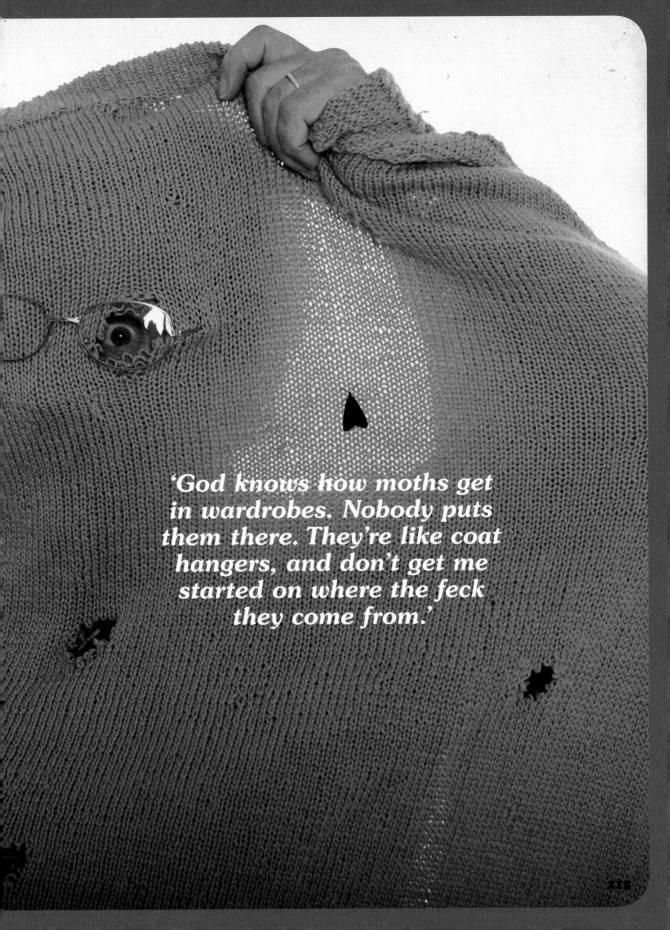

'God knows how moths get in wardrobes. Nobody puts them there. They're like coat hangers, and don't get me started on where the feck they come from.'

MOUSTACHES

There are four sorts of moustache:

- **The Professor**
- **The Dictator**
- **The Stripper**
- **The Grandmother**

None of them inspire confidence.
A moustache without a beard is slightly better
than those weird beards-without-a-moustache that
Scandinavian chemists have so it looks like they
ought to be on a little toadstool with a fishing rod,
but you really want both parts of the set if you
want to look the full ticket.

The Professor

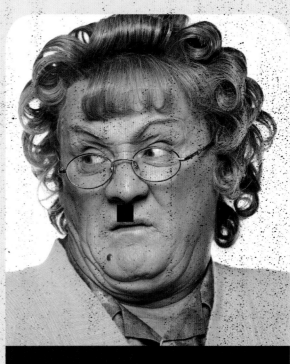

The Dictator

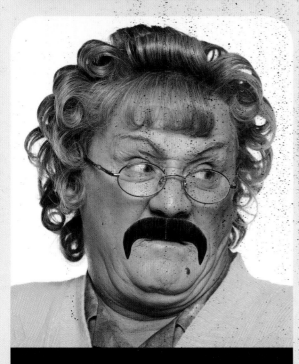

The Stripper

The Grandmother

IS FOR...

NOLANS, THE

If you ask me (and you are, because there's nobody else here, because Dermot's doing his leaflets and Grandad's in for a routine scrape), there have never been *any finer musicians* to come out of Ireland than The Nolans.

They did everything those Spice Girls did but remembered to match their outfits.

That's the bare minimum you need from a musical group: matching slacks. Otherwise how do I know who's singing and who's doing the meat raffle? Basic manners.

Coleen (the drummer) was my favourite. And then there was Belinda, Margaret, Bernard, other Coleen, Babs, Fiona, Maggie, Maureen, Joan, Gertie, 'T-Bone', Peggy, and last and least, their ugly brother who played the guitar.

I'm one of their biggest fans. I have met Joan Nolan (I could tell by her name badge, because she was working in Aldi at the time), and I have seen them live four times (on the television), unless I'm thinking of The Corrs.

If you asked me what their best record was, I'd tell you. 'Cause that's an easy one. *The Best of The Nolans.* It's written on the front. Brilliant record. Every song on it is a hit, unlike some records I could name. (Unless I am thinking of The Corrs, of course. Then their best record would be *The Best of The Corrs*, which is probably brilliant too.)

NORMANS, THE

Cathy told me I should get a bit of history in here. She said, 'Do the Tudors or the Normans or something.' I told her I know nothing about the Tudors, except that they moved out when their Betty found herself up Bun Street without a Daddy.

I do know a bit about the Normans, though. Funny pair. No one ever really knew if they were brothers or what. (You know what.) They lived in a house in Donnybrook which was absolutely jam-packed with stuff. They were hoarders before it was fashionable to keep everything and go on the telly to get some of it thrown away.

One-Eyed Norman was the Norman with one eye, and Just Plain Norman had two.

One-Eyed Norman lost his other eye in a bet (if you believe some of the stories) or in a fight (if you believe the others) or in a supermarket (if you believe Winnie).

Didn't we all think they were very grand? Always strolling around town in their cravats, that day's newspapers under their arms, with their dog, who was also called Norman.

And yet nobody went in the house. Everybody thought they must have a fortune stashed away in there. The windows were always steamed up, but Just Plain Norman always said that was because One-Eyed Norman liked boiling water. It was his hobby. The place was covered in kettles and saucepans, they said.

Well, eventually poor old One-Eye succumbed to the lurgy and passed away. And Just Plain Norman couldn't cope on his own, so he went into a nursing home. And because I was such a pillar of the community and used to buy pet food for Dog Norman whenever I was in Superquinn, Just Plain Norman asked me to do the house clearance.

I was made up, I tell you. A whole treasure trove to go through! This could be the making of us. What if they'd been collecting art or gilt and zirconium heirloom clown statuettes like out the back of the supplements?

MISSING

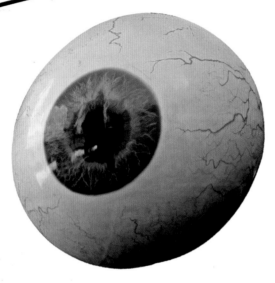

HAVE YOU SEEN THIS EYE?

LAST SEEN IN EITHER THE BETTING SHOP,
IN THAT FIGHT OUTSIDE THE PUB LAST WEEK,
OR CHECKING OUT THE SAUSAGES IN SUPERQUINN.
KEEP A WATCHFUL EYE OUT, WOULD YA?!

REWARD: A YEAR'S SUPPLY OF EYE-SPY BOOKS
ANY SIGHTINGS CALL ONE-EYED NORMAN
ON HIS EYE-PHONE: 999 1066

Was it feck.

It was like a rubbish dump in there. Once I'd thrown away the piles and piles of newspaper, all I found were:

- 38 kettles.

- A shiteload more cravats.

- A fridge full of motorbike parts.

- 'The Onion Family' – that's what it said on the lid – six onions, all with faces drawn on them and roots coming out their tops like you wouldn't believe. They must have been there years.

- A lifetime's supply of broken biscuits (all off).

- A trombone that had mice living in it.

- A sewing machine that had gone rusty with all the steam.

- A trunk full of folders marked 'IMPORTANT', all of which were full of photos of leopards.

- One-Eyed Norman's glass eye that he never wore.

- And – would you believe it? All the feckin' dog food I'd been buying them over the years.

The ungrateful buggers. Lord knows what Dog Norman was eating all that time. Sure it must have been either broken biscuits or mice. No wonder his coat was patchy.

Anyway, I cleared it all out (with a bit of help from Mark and Trevor and Grandad's old gas mask) and organized it into two piles in the front garden: rubbish and stuff for the auction. The rubbish pile was nearly as high as the house. The auction pile was a lot smaller. In fact, it was just a glass eye and a couple of cravats. So we binned the lot.

Two days later, the house fell down. The council said the damp had done for it, and it had only been the rubbish keeping the place up. Which goes to show you. Although I haven't a feckin' clue what it goes to show you, except that some people are batshit doolally.

And that's the history of the Normans.

NUCULAR POWER

You can tell that was a man's idea. Sticking their hot rods in things, exploding all over the shop and leaving a terrible mess no amount of scrubbing will get out. What was wrong with good, clean, old-fashioned power, like coal? And it's not caught on, I tell you. You can't buy anything nucular down the coke and fuel place. People still use coal fires, gas ovens, electric lights, and if anyone's got a nucular washing machine, I've not heard about it. (See Laundry.)

IS FOR...
OPPOSITES

OPPOSITES

A lot of a Mammy's wisdom comes from simply knowing the opposite of things. The opposite of shower-head crust is vinegar, so vinegar gets it off. The opposite of window smears is also vinegar, so vinegar gets them off too. The opposite of ants, it turns out (and nobody was more feckin' surprised than me, who thought it might be elephants), is also vinegar, so sprinkling some vinegar about will repel them, which certainly saves on calling the zoo every time the little feckers get in the sugar. And the opposite of chips-without-vinegar is vinegar as well, so I always keep some handy in case of a sudden emergency there.

Here are some of my favourite opposites, which you might find useful.

WASPS

V

VINEGAR

WASPS LIKE JAM. JAM IS THE OPPOSITE OF VINEGAR. SO A WASP STING CAN BE CURED WITH VINEGAR. ALSO ADD VINEGAR TO A SANDWICH IF YOU'VE PUT TOO MUCH JAM IN.

HOT COLD

V

If you burn yourself, pop a bag of frozen peas on the affected part. Also works for cooling a man's hot groin if you're not in the mood.

AN AGNES BROWN FIGHT

SHOE POLISH

VS

MILK

Shoe polish is black and milk is white, so if you get polish on a carpet, try rubbing in a pint of milk.

MILK VINEGAR

THE SMELL OF RANCID MILK CAN BE REMOVED FROM A CARPET WITH VINEGAR.

VINEGAR V GLADE

The smell of vinegar can be removed from a carpet by shoving a load of different Glade PlugIns into a four-socket extension cable, closing the door and not going in there for a week.

CAT SHIT V BLEACH

SHIT FROM NEXT-DOOR'S CAT CAN BE DEALT WITH WITH A SQUIRT OF BLEACH (FOR EXAMPLE, OVEN CLEANER). SIMPLY AIM THE BLEACH AT THE CAT AND SQUEEZE THE TRIGGER.

WALNUT V SCRATCHES

RUB A WALNUT ON WOODEN FURNITURE TO COVER SCRATCHES. AND THE REVERSE: REMOVE THE WALNUT FROM THE TOP OF A WALNUT WHIP BY SCRATCHING IT OFF WITH YOUR FINGERNAILS. OPPOSITES. SIMPLE.

ONIONS

V

STRAWBERRIES

TO AVOID TEARS WHEN CHOPPING ONIONS, STRING SOME STRAWBERRIES ROUND YOUR NECK (WHICH ARE PROBABLY THE OPPOSITE OF ONIONS).

FIGHT NIGHT

RED WINE

V

O'GRADY'S SPECIAL

When dealing with stains, white wine isn't the opposite of red wine, as it's still quite posh. The opposite of red wine is the standard 3-litre bottle of O'Grady's 9% discount special-strength cider. And if it won't lift the stain, have a glass of it yourself and you'll stop giving a feck.

FAT V THIN

Doing a pan full of sausages is a nightmare. They always spit and you end up with fat stains on your top. So simply lose some weight, and when you're a bit thinner, you'll have to buy new tops.

POSH

V

EVERYONE ELSE

If you're posh, everyone else thinks you're unbuckingbearable. Oh, hello, Hilliary. I didn't see you there.

IS FOR...

PANDAS
PENGUINS
PET CARE
PHILOSOPHY
PICKLE
PICNICS
PIES
PILES
PLUMBERS
POLITICS
POSTMEN
POWER CUTS
PRUNES
PUNK

PANDAS

Pandas are the priests of the animal world. Black and white, bone idle, and not likely to have any children on purpose.

Did you know, your panda lass gets frisky for three days a year. *Three feckin' days?* I've known women like that. You see them in the library, nibbling away at their crackerbreads and giving everyone the thin eye.

And your panda fella can't be bothered most of the time, even when Mrs Panda suddenly shows a bit of interest. Now, we've *all* met men like that. Some of us have married them, haven't we, Minnie O'Driscoll? (Not me, mind. Redser was more of a rabbit than a panda. I had to turn the heating off sometimes just so as he'd put some feckin' clothes on.)

It's as if pandas don't even fancy other pandas. Like they'd rather have a more interesting bear to have a bit of fumble and grumble with. One that wasn't so boring. One that was in colour. One that wasn't a feckin' vegetarian. It's no wonder the silly buggers are dying out.

Anything that'd rather sit around on its fat furry arse all day eating bits of fence than having a shag doesn't deserve to survive.

Tell you what: if they were at least tasty, like pigs, we'd have been breeding them and there'd be pandas everywhere. But no one wants a black-and-white sausage.

Fig. 1:
Black and white, sits on furry arse all day, doesn't shag, on the verge of extinction

Fig. 2:
Black and white, sits on furry arse all day, doesn't shag, on the verge of extinction

PENGUINS

What are they up to? It bothers me. There's millions of the feckers out there, scattered over the snow like little fishy commas. What are they doing? And why do we need so many of them? Normally when there's loads of something, it's because humans like to eat them. But we don't.

Can you believe that? We don't even eat them. Apparently the actual penguin content of those chocolate biscuits is so small as to be almost insignificant. I looked at the list on the back of the wrapper and it's almost all sugar, you know, the usual way they cover up skimping on quality ingredients.

People act like penguins are a big deal. There's kids' books and films and nature documentaries and that, but I don't know anyone who's ever met one. You think there'd be more stuff about crows, and starlings, and birds we actually have round us, but no, it's penguins, penguins, penguins. I've had a ball of fat hanging in the garden for three years and never seen a single penguin. (It's not a ball of fat as such, but I sometimes throw leftover bacon out and it gets caught on the whirligig.)

I think it's because they're black and white, and people like that. Think about how nice people are to pandas, no matter how annoying they are (see Pandas). And badgers are no better. You get cut a lot of slack if you're black and white. Look at nuns.

According to this film Rory made me watch, which I think was narrated by God, so it's pretty reliable, penguins are monogramous creatures, meaning they only breed with one partner. But how do we know? They all look the feckin' same. Who's checking which one's with which? Scientists? Feckin' layabouts (see Sonar System). Out there, poking their noses in, checking penguins aren't playing the field. Have you seen the conditions these penguins live in? Freezing ice, no shelter, rotten fish to eat. And you're making sure they're not having a bit of flipper-over on the side. Give the weird little feckers a break. Let them have their fun.

Ah, but that's scientists for you. You'd think they'd find something proper to do, like making a sink brush that'll get batter off a whisk.

'Apparently the actual penguin content of those chocolate biscuits is so small as to be almost insignificant'

PET CARE

Pets are a great way to teach kids about death, almost as good as making them take the plate of picnic eggs round at a wake.

PET CARE ASSOCIATION

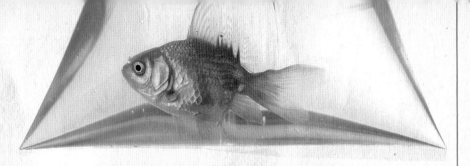

The best pets
are those goldfish...

...in a sandwich bag that you win at the fair. They're usually dead by the time the coconut's hit the ground, so you get all the fun of burying it without any of the fuss of getting to know it. Plus you get a free sandwich bag.

NEXT BEST ARE GERBILS OR HAMSTERS

They've been designed by God to last about as long as a child's attention span.

Think of pets like those novelty duvet covers with all cartoon characters on them: kiddies are mad for them, so you splash out, and then they go off the whole feckin' idea and start asking for a different one. Take my advice: don't bother.

And no matter how much the nippers moan, don't

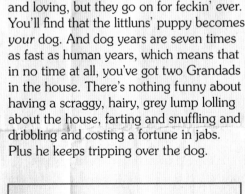

cave in and buy a dog. They may be loyal and loving, but they go on for feckin' ever. You'll find that the littluns' puppy becomes *your* dog. And dog years are seven times as fast as human years, which means that in no time at all, you've got two Grandads in the house. There's nothing funny about having a scraggy, hairy, grey lump lolling about the house, farting and snuffling and dribbling and costing a fortune in jabs. Plus he keeps tripping over the dog.

> *Remember:*
> A dog, like that jar of piccalilli at the back of the tins cupboard, is for life, not just for Christmas.

FOR MORE INFORMATION CALL 672156 NOW

Most pets do die* and depending on size,
you have to do something about it. Here's a guide.

The Mammy
Standard Pet Disposal Chart

Type 1	Type 2	Type 3
Goldfish	**Hamster/ gerbil**	**Guinea pig/ rabbit**

Grade	Grade	Grade
Very easy	Easy	Reasonably easy
Method of Disposal	Method of Disposal	Method of Disposal
Flush down lavatory. Fuss free. Kids barely notice. Win another at the fair within a year, give it the same name. Ideal pet.	Put in matchbox. Bury in garden with lolly stick cross. Name on lolly stick, otherwise will be forgotten. Replace if can be arsed.	Shoebox in garden. Kids put up sad crayon drawings on fridge for a week, then forget they ever had it. Can be replaced within a month.

Type 4	Type 5	Type 6
Cat/ small dog	**Large dog/ pony**	**Horse**

Grade	Grade	Grade
Quite hard	Hard	Feckin' impossible
Method of Disposal	Method of Disposal	Method of Disposal
Grocery box burial in hole that takes two people half an hour with a spade. Kids remember animal fondly, but not too sad.	Full burial that requires light plant hire. Report to authorities. Elaborate lies to children that 'Rover's gone to live on a lovely farm' to soften the blow.	Funeral pyre like a maharajah. Neighbours annoyed by smoke. Police investigate. Remember to take washing in. Kids distracted with big box of sparklers.

*I say most, because Deirdra Grainger says the tortoise she's got has been in the family four generations. I'm pretty sure it will die one day, but it hasn't yet.

"Garfield." © Paws. Used by Permission.

PHILOSOPHY

Philosophy is what you think. Actually, it's usually what other people think.

I know what I think: you can do too much thinking. It's not good to think too hard about some things.

Like the time when Rory was young and asked me how many places there were in the world. I did what every good Mammy does when a nipper asks them something they can't answer, and said, 'That's a good question.'

But God knows I lay awake for three nights trying to add them up. Nearly drove me mad. And a few days later, Rory says to me, 'Mammy – when you come to think about it, there's loads of places just in your own mouth.' That's when I stopped giving him that cheap cough medicine.

245

PICKLE

There's nothing that's not better with a bit of pickle. I bet you could put it on gangrene and it'd do some good.

You can make your own pickle, just like you can make your own feckin' house if you want to. It takes fuckin' ages, and the Londis does it for loose change, so you'd have to be mentally ill or medically bored to even think about it. There's proper stuff needs doing, like laundry (see Laundry).

Pickle is a preserve, which means you can leave it at the back of the cupboard until it starts pushing away at the lid, wanting to get out, which is probably a safe time to throw it away.

When your man dug down into the basement of the pyramids and unlocked the big scary brass pharaoh coffins, he found some jars of stuff that hadn't been opened for thousands of years. I've no idea what it was, but it's bound to have been pickle, because pickle's job is to sit unopened for as long as possible. Everything else gets eaten.

The oldest jar of pickle at the back of my cupboard is some onion chutney I never got on with, which has a tie-in competition for some Batman film or other, with Robin in. It might have gone off, but I don't want to open it because it's steamed up the glass and who knows what sort of state it's in.

I'm keeping it, you know, just in case someone fancies some. I wouldn't want to be caught short.

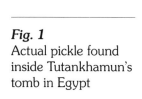

Fig. 1
Actual pickle found inside Tutankhamun's tomb in Egypt

PICNICS

Eating outdoors like a tramp. You can come inside and eat at a proper table we got on the never-never and almost broke us.

I didn't go without proper cheese for the best part of two years so you can squat on a sheet and attract ants. Get indoors. We'll open the fanlight if you're gasping for fresh air. You're not an animal.

PIES

I've made my fair share of pies – well, I've bought them from Foley's – and I'll tell you one ingredient that has absolutely no feckin' place whatsoever in a pie: crockery.

But didn't Cathy take me for a birthday lunch at some hoity-toity new pub with tables as thick as a tombstone and wooden coasters – and they'd only gone and taken a perfectly good steak and kidney pie and made the bottom half out of a feckin' china dish. It wasn't a pie, it was a lid resting on the top of some sauce. That's feckin' cheating, that is. I nearly broke my teeth before I realized.

When I buy a mug, I don't expect it to be made of pastry, and I expect the same courtesy in return. Dossers.

Anatomy of a Proper Pie

Lid
(made from pastry)

Base
(made from pastry*)
***not feckin' crockery**

Side
(made from pastry)

PILES

Oh my godfather's auntie, don't talk to me about piles. I've suffered arsegrapes in bunches the size of a grown man's fist. No idea why: it's not like I spend my whole time sitting on radiators.

And I've only had six or seven kids. I haven't really pushed the boat out. (Although giving birth to Dermot felt like pushing a feckin' boat out.)

Me, I go the usual route: cream. There's plenty you can buy. One tip: don't keep it next to the toothpaste. You only need to reach for it without your glasses on and get the wrong tube once to learn a bucking harsh lesson: piles don't like anything minty. Jaysus, the sting. I was leaping around that bathroom like a borstal cat on bonfire night.

'Don't keep the cream next to the toothpaste… Piles don't like anything minty.'

Redser was a martyr to his piles. At one point, he wouldn't sit at the dinner table unless the spare tyre for the wheelbarrow was on his seat. He'd never use ointments or whatnot, he didn't trust anything that came out of a tube (till the day he passed, he cleaned his teeth with mint sauce). But he had developed his own medically proven technique to prevent unnecessary pile discomfort: he pushed them back up his arse with his thumb. He was practical like that.

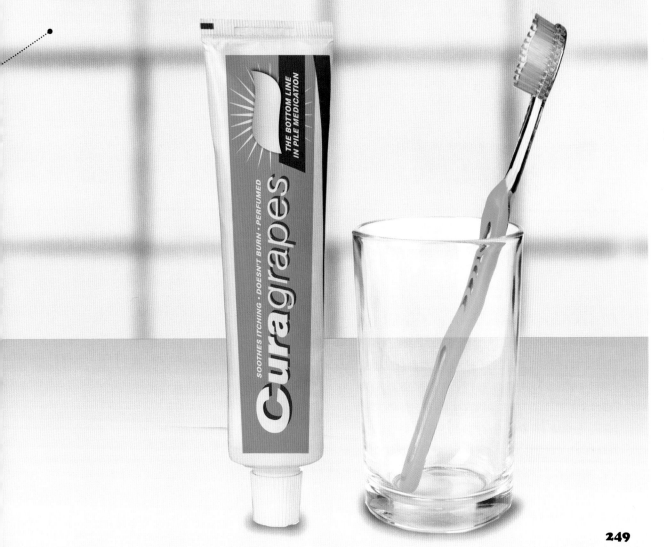

SOOTHES ITCHING · DOESN'T BURN · PERFUMED

Curagrapes

THE BOTTOM LINE IN PILE MEDICATION

PLUMBERS

Retirement, Cider, Church, Plumbers

Plumbers' bills are a feckin' shocker. But if you offer to pay in cash, they often lower the bill. If you offer to pay in loose change from the penny jar, you'll be surprised how much they'll knock off. Just to save their backs.

POLITICS

Some people say you shouldn't vote because politicians are all the feckin' same, but I think that's shocking. People died for your vote. It's your duty, and every politician is different.

Some of them have baldy heads, and some of them have eyes like a dead mole, and some of them look like they're going to sell you a hoover.

Generally, I vote for the nicest looking fella. And if it's a woman, I vote for the plainest one. She should have better things on her mind than lipstick. And that's what they call demonocracy.

Sometimes I've not noticed there's an election coming up and I get in the voting booth and I haven't got a Scooby Doo what they look like, and there's no pictures on the form. (How hard would that be? Jaysus.) If that's the case, I try making a face out of the letters of their name, and make my mind up that way. I've been in there hours, drawing, moving the letters round. I've had to ask for a second feckin' pencil.

Over here, the only people who talk about politics are the tourists. You won't catch the locals doing it. You start talking politics round here and you might as well have just offered free money to anyone willing to start a feckin' great fight. But I think that's one of the things that keeps us a happy lot. Why would you want to stand around arguing with people about a load of things you're never going to agree on, when you can save all that for conversations with Hilliary? It's much more fun.

HOW TO CHOOSE THE RIGHT CANDIDATE

Rank options in order of preference

✗	**IS HE NICE LOOKING?** The best-looking fella always gets my vote	
	IS SHE PLAIN? She should have better things on her mind than lipstick	
	MAKE A FACE FROM THEIR NAME If there are no pictures	
	DOES	

POSTMEN

There's something, I don't know, 'erotic' about a milkman, but nobody ever had an affair with the postman.

I've been thinking about this all day, and I wonder if it isn't that the milkman is a bringer of promise (cup of milky tea, cheese on toast, cherry yoghurt), while the postman only brings bills and reminders that every year takes you one step closer to the grave. But when you think about it, what is a milkman but a postman with a very limited repertoire?

I say it's time for people to start having it away with the postman. I wouldn't recommend the potato man, though. He's got hands like the hull of a fishing smack. It'd be like getting rubbed down with a barnacled plank. I imagine. I wouldn't know. No, you feck off.

The Milkman
'Bringer of Promise'
(milky tea, cheese on toast and cherry yoghurt)

The Postman
'Bringer of Bills'

POWER CUTS

Power cuts are one of those things you don't get any more, like hedgehogs (see Hedgehogs) or flashers or spivs. Pity, really, because didn't we have a lot of fun when the lights went out? I reckon a better power supply is to blame for the childbirth rate falling in Ireland. If it has.

Sure, candle sales must have feckin' plummeted since the power started staying on. What with church attendances falling too. If they have. (I've not checked. I've not got time. I've got a feckin' book to write.)

Course, one thing you can do, if you don't get the proper power cuts any more, is make your own entertainment by causing a power cut. If your house is anything like mine, it will have been wired by Redser back in the 1970s, and you don't need to do much to blow a fuse. I only have to put the kettle on when the plug isn't expecting it for the entire house to go dark and a smell like hot dogs to come out of the sockets (I mean, like a schnauzer in a locked car, not the sausage-based snack).

Kids these days get the proper hump if there's a power cut. Not because the TV's gone off, either. No. It's all their feckin' phones and chargers and the feckin' fi-wi. You leave them without a glowing rectangle in their hands and they think the world's ended.

In the event of a power cut

Well, let me tell you youngsters, there's loads you can do during a power cut. (Apart from that. That's for when you're older.) Use your imagination. You can:

- Go looking for candles
- Go looking for a torch
- Go looking for batteries for the torch

- Realize you can't see anything in the cupboard under the stairs where the batteries usually are
- Go looking for the other torch to help you look for the batteries for the first torch

- Find a paraffin lamp
- Go looking for some paraffin
- Find a bottle of something that might be paraffin
- Take the risk

- Find out it's not paraffin but screen wash
- Throw the paraffin lamp away
- Start pulling batteries out of other things

- Realize one of the things you pulled the batteries out of was the other torch
- Put the batteries from the other torch in the first torch
- Find out the batteries don't work

By this time, the power should have come back on. If not, you can all sing a rude song or, if the nippers are getting restless, tell them a ghost story ('The Shining' is quite good). That usually shuts them up.

*'Kids these days...
You leave them without
a glowing rectangle in
their hands and they think
the world's ended.'*

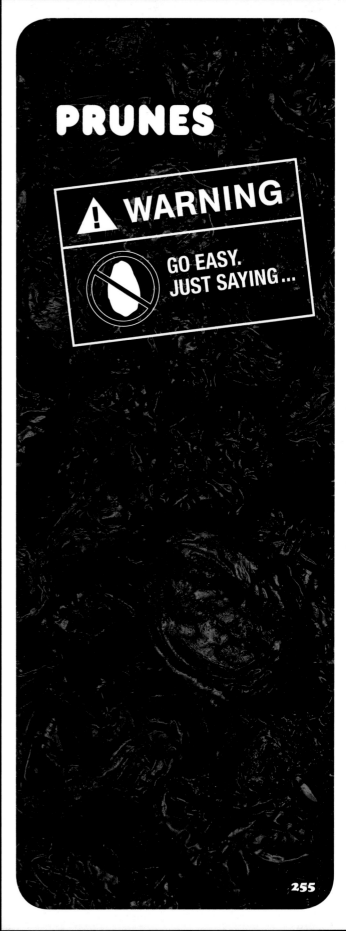

PRUNES

⚠ WARNING

🚫 GO EASY.
JUST SAYING...

PUNK

Now, I like a sing-song as much as the next man dressed as a woman. All the old favourites – 'Whiskey in the Jar', 'Danny Boy', 'Get Up (I Feel Like Being a) Sex Machine' – but I draw the line at anything that involves spitting.

I remember punk. You might think I'm too young to, but I do. I remember seeing them all slouching about on street corners with their bright-pink hair and their faces all covered in pins like they were the notice board outside St Saviour's.

You'd think they'd all joined a club for people who shout instead of having baths. Mucky lot. And some of the disgusting slogans they'd felt-tipped on to the backs of their jackets. You wouldn't believe the feckin' language.

I remember when Mark was a teenager, he went through a bit of a punky phase. It started with the denim jacket. Then these big boots that, side-on, made him look like a golf club. And then he came home with his head shaved clean, slumping and snarling his lip. He looked like that cheap mannequin they had in the Sally Army shop window that melted.

One day he told me he was off to a concert in town. I said, 'That's nice, son. Who is it? Anyone we know? James Galway, is it? That nice Dana?' He said, 'No, Ma. It's The Unbelievable Shits of Fascist Mucus.' I said, 'Would you mind repeating that? But maybe outside in the garden where I can pretend I didn't feckin' hear you right?'

Anyway, no son of mine was going to see The Unbelievable Shits of Fascist Mucus unprotected. Anything could have happened to him.

So I went with him.

YOU WOULDN'T beLieve the feckiN'

LANGUAGE

MUCUS ENTERTAINMENT
PRESENTS

The UNbelievable
ShiTS Of FaSciST MUCUS

KEEP TICKET FOR ADMISSION INTO CONCERT

NO REFUNDS | NO REFUNDS | 9.00pm | '834578

MUCUS ENTERTAINMENT WORLDWIDE

KEEP TICKET FOR
ADMISSION INTO CONCERT

9.00pm | 83457

What a feckin' racket. Screaming and shouting.
I couldn't work out what they were so cross
about. Perhaps it was the uncomfortable boots.
God knows, I've made a fair fuss when a pair
of shoes has bitten me heels.

And I couldn't hear a word of what they were
singing. It might have been the hanky I had
stuffed in each ear.

But I looked around me at all these sweaty yobs
throwing themselves at each other and hawking
up snot, and it looked like something from one
of those films Redser used to like where all the
inmates in a borstal go berserk and smash up the
canteen. And I thought to myself, I'm not having
our Mark getting into this. I'd rather he took up
circus skills like a proper clown, or, God forbid,
joined the Church.

I had to stop him. But a Mammy can fight a
teenager all she likes. She's like the wind trying
to blow the man's coat off in that Eejit's Fable.
Blow and blow and blow, you'll not get a man
to do what you want; believe me. I've tried.
You'll end up with egg on your face. Or worse.

And that's when it came to me. What makes
the man in the Eejit's Fable take his coat off?
The sun. Shining away like the big happy
boiling-hot bastard he is.

Mark said to me afterwards, 'So what did you
reckon, Mammy?' And I said, 'Son, those
Unbelievable Shits of yours were absolutely
fan-feckin'-tastic.' Well, you could have scraped
his chin off the pavement with a fish slice.
'I loved them. Smashing lads. I think I'll just pop
round the back of the theatre and invite them
all over to tea.'

'No, Mammy!' he said. 'Don't do that!'

But it was too late for that.

If my son was going to have
the punk wiped off his face,
I had to turn the embarrassment
up to eleven.

And that's how it came to be that all four members of The Unbelievable Shits of Fascist Mucus (Ted Menace, Zero Hope, Fists Vomit and Julian Prosser-Anarchy, whose dad it turned out owned the land they built the bus station on, would you believe?) sat round the kitchen table with me and Mark and had a lovely cup of tea. I was as nice as pie, beaming like a nun.

The band were all very quiet and confused. And Mark was about as purple as I've seen anyone since Deirdre Regan gave birth to triplets in the revolving doors at Boyers.

That was the last time Mark listened to any punk. He was devastated after that, and moved on to Olivia Newton-John. Nice, clean-living lass next door.

Mind you, things took a turn again when he got into the New Romantics. The clothes! He looked like David Essex going to a fancy-dress party as a carnival float. So, obviously, Mammy started dressing like that Boyd George. Put the dampeners on that one.

I'm telling you: it never fails. Embarrassment is nine-tenths of the law.

After punk there was the New Romantics
Dressing like Boyd George soon put him off

IS FOR...

QUILTS, CONTINENTAL

I've got a wicker basket full of these, and that's what you'll get if you ask for a duvet round my house.

I accepted new foreign blankets once; I'm not changing again, even if we are in the euro now.

IS FOR...
RADIATORS
RAP
RELATIVITY

RADIATORS
AND HOW TO GET BEHIND THEM

If anything goes missing in my place, it's behind the radiator.

Window keys, odd socks, love letters, coupons, mobile phones, LP records, birth certificates, much-loved pictures that used to hang above the radiator, Grandad's hat, Grandad's hand. And once they're down there, no amount of diddling with a knitting needle will get them out.

They just stay there, getting warm, and then cold, and then warm, and then cold, day after day. I made a list so I wouldn't keep looking for them, but unfortunately it fell behind the radiator. The only answer is to remove the radiator, remove the items and then replace the radiator, but that still leaves you with a radiator for more stuff to fall behind. Why can't they make radiators with two big holes in? Maybe with gloves you can reach through, like they have in nucular reactors. How hard can it be? Honestly. But no, they're too busy pretending to go to the moon. Bloody men.

WHAT LIES BEHIND …

DANIEL O'DONNELL
a picture of

CRAP

Rap has two things missing. Firstly, there's a 'c' missing from the front of its name.

Secondly, it's what music would be like if you took the music out. I hear it coming out of cars and shops and under the bedroom doors (when the kids were going through the pimples-and-feck-off stage) and it's a dreadful feckin' racket.

Sounds like a fight's about to kick off in a steelworks. But I tell you something: no matter how much I don't like it, it does remind me of being a youngster myself, and that's no bad thing.

I remember when I was a teenager, I used to hide in my room – or as my dad used to call it, The Coal Shed – and I used to play music that my old dad hated something terrible. And he'd shout up at me to 'shut that rubbish the feck up' and 'turn that racket the feck down' and 'what's that God-awful feckin' noise' and 'don't you feckin' know who I am?' Always bawling and thumping the ceiling with a broom, he was.

And rap reminds me of that. Because it sounds like they've taken my dad's shouting and bawling and made that the feckin' song.

RELATIVITY

Your man Alfred Einstein worked this out, and I can't make head nor tail of it. Even the greatest mind of all time couldn't make it so anyone could actually follow it, which is next to feckin' pointless.

But that's how it is with relatives. They make no feckin' sense.

I'm apparently related to Hilliary. I think it's something to do with Newton's first in-law, which goes something like 'any action has an equal and opposite over-reaction'. He might never have been the same since that blow on the head, but he got that spot on.

Relativity:
Relatives – they make
no feckin' sense

IS FOR...

SAUSAGES
SELLOTAPE
SHAKESPEARE
SHOPPING TROLLEYS
SHORTS
SNEEZING
SONAR SYSTEM, THE
SPIDERS
SPORT
SUITCASE CONTAINING
ALL THE IMPORTANT STUFF, THE
SWEARING*

*BUT MAINLY SAUSAGES

SAUSAGES

Sausages are the corner of any diet. And you know how it is with corners: some people's are filled with the most shocking muck.

You hear tell about butchers and supermarkets trying to get away with murder, stuffing their sausages with all the parts of the animal nobody wants: pig's lips, cow's bollocks, sheep's laps. Hooves from poor factory animals that shouldn't have hooves, like ducks.

The day I serve my children a duck-hoof sausage is the day you can bury me in an unbuttoned cardigan.

But don't worry, you can tell a quality sausage by how it looks.

A nice healthy sausage should be as straight as a stick of seaside rock and bright pink too. And good and narrow so you can fit plenty on the plate. You're looking for a shop that'll sell you about 40 or so of them in a standard €4 packet. Big clear number on the bag: 40. That's a healthy big number that is. To show the quality.

I've seen the filth Hilliary serves her lot. Bought from a farmer's market, she says. Pudgy great things, all gnarled like a goblin's thumb, speckled with what look like mouse droppings and bits off the floor.

Well, no wonder. I've seen the dirt under a farmer's fingernails.

And she serves you up one feckin' sausage each. For fuck's sake. *That woman has no pride.* Not that I'd want to eat two. The things are cold by the time I've gone through them with a fork picking the black bits out. She says it's herbs, but herbs have got as much business being in a sausage as they have in a feckin' crisp, and she's tried that on me before too.

Sausages are meant to be made of meat, not filled with bits of vegetable. That's cheating. And those farmers must have seen her coming a mile off.

Mammy's guide to
THE PERFECT SAUSAGE

Fig. 1
The perfect sausage

- Bright pink
- Poker straight
- Comes in packs of 40

MAMMY APPROVED · MAMMY APPROVED ·

⟵ *As straight as a stick of rock* ⟶

Fig. 2
Hilliary's Farmer's Market sausage

- Pudgy, fat things
- Gnarly like a goblin's thumb
- Look like they contain mouse droppings and bits of floor

Almost any recipe can be improved by the addition of some sausages. Here are some of my favourites:

Main Meals

- Sausage casserole with peas and more sausages
- Turduckenages (a turkey stuffed with a duck stuffed with a chicken stuffed with sausages)
- Yard-o'-sausages
- Sausages served with sausage mash (mashed sausages)

Light Snacks

- Boiled egg with sausage soldiers
- Sausage cheese on toast
- Cup of tea with side-sausage

Diet Meals

- Low-calorie miso soup with 12 (twelve) Superquinn sausages eaten straight off the grill
- Breadless no-sausage sandwich (served with sausages)

Kids' Menu

- Mashed potato man with sausage 'fists'
- Mammy's Sausage Shapes
  (shapes: sausage, cigar, severed finger)

And if you're trying to impress a guest, you can insist a plate of sausages are some of them Heston Bloomingtall-style vegetables made out of minced meat you see on the telly. I said mine were asparagus spears and got away with it! (Neither of us had ever seen an asparagus spear, mind.)

What's more, sausages have dozens of household uses, whether it's sizing up an engagement ring, cleaning the dirt off your Venetian blinds or keeping your toes apart when painting your nails. I don't think there's anything you can't do with a sausage. I know plenty of women who'd swap their husband for a sausage, if it could hang shelves. (Science will make this happen one day, you mark my words.)

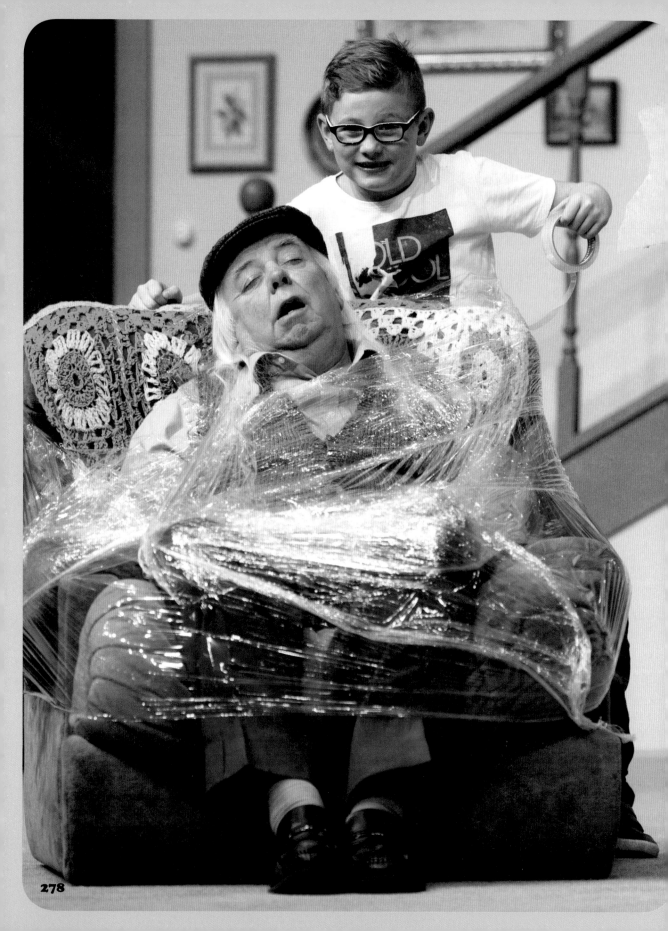

SELLOTAPE

Forget the computer. Forget the printing press. Forget the comestible intention engine, or whatever it's called. The greatest invention of all time is Sellotape. Part miracle, part mystery. It's a bit like the Holy Trinity, but stickier.

Everyone's got a roll or two of Sellotape in the house. And no one knows where.

That's why you have to go out and buy another roll of Sellotape – or, like me, keep one hidden. (No, I'm not feckin' tell you where. My kids might read this, and then my secret Sellotape's gone for a feckin' burton, just like my lucky jar full of sherbet lemons did.)

Honestly, the list of things I've fixed with Sellotape could fill a book on its own – pictures on the wall, the guttering, the car, a bow tie on Dermot – if you use enough of it, you can fix anything. After that runaway milk float came through her front window one morning, Aisling O'Sullivan put most of her house back together with it. It's still intact now. Although it's attracted a devil of a lot of fluff.

When you're wrapping a present, you can cut bits of it to length and stick them to the furniture, ready to use, so it looks like the table's a snake shedding its skin. Always remember where you've put them, though. I've accidentally taped my drawers shut before. (Kitchen drawers, you filthy-minded sod. I wouldn't use Sellotape on my undies, because I don't want to risk unwanted hair removal. Though it is good for hair removal, if you've come to the end of a 400-pack of waxing strips, and you've the patience.)

Sellotape has dozens of other uses, apart from sticking things together and yanking at your ingrowing private hair.

See overleaf for chart >

Fig. 1
Man's greatest invention:
Sellotape

ALTERNATIVE USES FOR **SELLOTAPE**

Key: [ ] = Sellotape

Clean-up Gloves

You can wrap it round the kids' hands and make them crawl all over the floor to pick the feathers up if Grandad bites a hole in his pillow having that dream about being a jackal.

First Aid

You can use it as a plaster, and it's much cheaper than some of the posh ones you can get with Postman Pat on them.

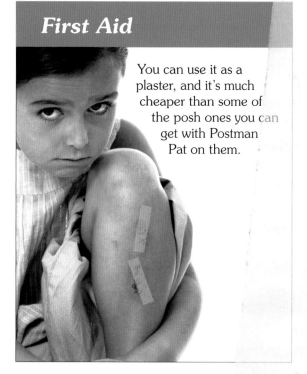

Glass Repair

Layer up enough of it and you can replace the broken lenses in reading glasses.* Although your *Woman's Way* might still look a bit blurred on one side.

* (And don't try it for contact lenses: Maureen Fagan's daughter nearly went blind.)

Nail Care

If you've run out of nail gloss, cut little fingernail-shaped bits out and stick them on the end of your fingers. No one'll notice the difference.

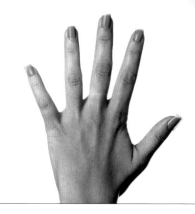

Silencer

You can silence a screaming kid with it. Some people say that's a bit cruel, but it's kinder than superglue.

Book Covers

You can use it to cover the kids' schoolbooks if you haven't got that nice cling film stuff and you don't want to peel any more wallpaper out of the cupboard under the stairs.

Ornaments

If you're round Hilliary's house and you accidentally break a cut-glass swan ornament, a quick bit of Mammy origami with a length of Sellotape will get you a replacement she won't notice for at least six months. (She doesn't do her own dusting, so it'll only be when her cleaner walks out that she finds out.)

Christmas Decorations

You can make pretty good Christmas decorations out of scrunched-up balls of Sellotape.

Although, when the tree lights get hot, it can smell a bit like when Donal Whelan lost his house and had to run his dental practice from the room above the spare tyre place.

Emergency Hamster

Best of all, Sellotape is feckin' brilliant for making an emergency hamster. Scrunch a load of it up into a little hamster shape and roll it round the floor after you've cut the kiddies' hair, and bingo! You've got an emergency hamster. (You know, for when the one your boy brought home from school to look after in the holidays gets a bit, well, forgotten about under the stairs, and you have to take it back on the first day of term with a smile on your face and hope the blame lands on the next kid who takes the little fecker home.)

Finding the feckin' end of a roll of Sellotape is the hard bit, of course. It's very much the clitoris of household stationery. Which is why a woman can find it first time, while a man can stand there rubbing it and worrying at it for ages, getting more and more pissed off, while his wife gets bored and sighs quite a lot before eventually batting it out of his hands and saying, *'It's OK, I'll feckin' do it myself.'*

SHAKESPEARE

He's meant to be the best writer there ever was, but nobody can understand a word he's on about.

They pretend, but they can't. It's all back to front and upside down and with extra t's on the end of the words and it doesn't even rhyme most of the time.

I'm not calling myself a great writer – my L's look like 7's – but I can turn out a note for the milkman and be sure that he'll get my gist and, next morning, my doorstep will have an extra yoghurt on it. Shakespeare's milkman must have gone feckin' spare trying to work out what he was after. Nobody ever thinks of the milkmen, do they? (See Postmen.)

What the feck art thou going on about?

SHOPPING TROLLEYS

Shopping trolleys are pretty much giant metal puppies. If you don't housetrain them as soon as you come into contact with them, you're in the shite.

And you're setting yourself up for a whole shedload of bad behaviour and embarrassment in a public place.

Get on top of them, I'm telling you. (Not literally – that'd look weird. Like you were a huge baby. No one wants to look like a huge baby. Except on certain specialist websites. Or so I'm told. I haven't looked meself.)

If you reckon a shopping trolley's never going to behave, send it back to the pen. There's plenty more shopping trolleys in the sea (and the canal, come to that). But if you think you can tame it, then tuck in. Game on.

Shopping trolleys were invented in the 1950s by some gobdaw who wanted to waste everyone's lives trying to control an uncontrollable force. Like trying to nail jelly to a moving ceiling, but half as much fun. (Not even that, to be honest.)

SHORTS
Trousers for perverts.

SNEEZING

Sneezing is God's way of helping you silence Hilliary. If you're a good enough aim, you can make her leave altogether. That's why we say 'Bless you' after someone sneezes: to give thanks to the Lord for making Hilliary shut up and feck off.

It's also God's way of making you stay indoors, if you're a hayfever sufferer, like poor Cathy. About half the year the miserable thing sits there sniffling and sneezing, with a face like she's rubbed an extra-hot pizza over it, dripping with melted goo, eyes like pepperoni circles.

I've tried everything: stuff from the chemist's, honey in her tea, earplugs up each nostril, telling her to shut the feck up – none of it works. I always keep a tissue up my sleeve (it's part of a Mammy's uniform) but Cathy'd need a bucking great batwing jacket to keep the amount of tissues she needs up her sleeves. I suggested to her that she run a belt through a box of tissues and keep it round her waist at all times, but she reckoned it'd make her look like a toilet wall. I said, if it's good enough for Lady Gaga, it's good enough for you.

If you're lucky – *really lucky* – you'll get what Biddy Whelan had, the jammy sod. Every time she sneezed, *she had an organism.*

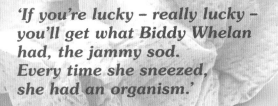

'If you're lucky – really lucky – you'll get what Biddy Whelan had, the jammy sod. Every time she sneezed, she had an organism.'

Yes. I tell you. She was forever beating her rug. She even went on holiday once to a gypsum plant in Cork. Tried to pretend to her old man it was a mix-up at the travel agent's. But I knew what she was up to. Lucky beggar.

MAMMY'S SNEEZE CHART

	The Controlled Explosion	**Small, tightly contained within the sneezer.** Very quiet. Common among mousy women.
	The Nice Surprise	**A proper little squirt,** but one which the sneezer wasn't expecting. Always leaves them smiling and looking like they've just left the pictures and are pleased to find it's still light outside.
	The Sambuca	**Pretty strong.** Leaves you shuddering slightly and leaning on something to get yourself back together. The ideal sneeze for a young couple on a first date.
	The Blow to the Head	**A real thumper.** Not the nice sort, though. The sort that makes you bend double. Can also have consequences for the woman who's carried a child to full term. Awkward on the bus.
	The Train Crash	**Disastrous.** You can feel it coming a mile off. The fecker gets nearer and nearer, and there's nothing you can do about it. Then it arrives, with an almighty wallop. I've lost false teeth this way.
	The Silverback	**Men only. A giant, roaring fuss that can be heard streets away.** It might sound like they've just coughed up one of their own legs, but it's just a sneeze. Yet they have to make such a feckin' song and dance about it. It's their noses' way of saying, 'HELLO. I'M OVER HERE.' They do the same with farts and burps. It's all a competition for them. I'm the biggest, I'm the loudest, I can pee the highest. Men are like kids who've just noticed they've got a fully-grown body and want to find out what they can get out of it. Usually noise.

There's all sorts of other interesting facts about sneezing, like how fast a sneeze comes out, and how fish sneeze, and how you can't sneeze with your eyes open.

But they're not in this book.

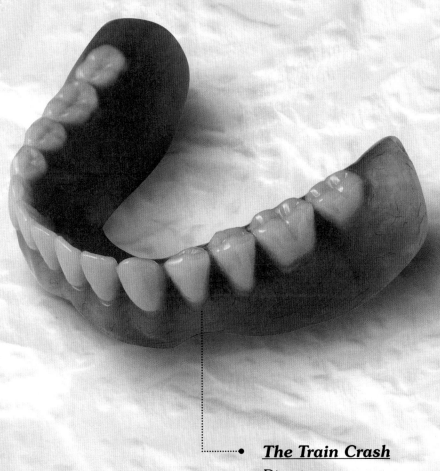

• **_The Train Crash_**
Disastrous.

SONAR SYSTEM, THE

What is the Sonar System?

When you write an address on a postcard or a letter to the council complaining about the noise the new bin lorries make now they're doing all sorts of plastic lids (and I don't care if you are taking milk caps and yoghurt pots, you can do it without sounding like the crack of feckin' doom, and that's not even mentioning all the feckin' leaflets I've been sent about the new recycling rules, which have gone straight in the kitchen bin – no, you feckin' sort it), you put the address in an order, don't you?

Name, house, road, town, city, county, and sometimes country, then you stop.If you didn't stop, and kept going, you'd find yourself doing the name of your planet (mine's Earth) and then, before 'Universe' and 'Space', you'd write 'The Sonar System'. And that's what the Sonar System is. It's where we are in space. 'Sonar', from the Roman word *'sonarus'*, meaning 'sonar', which is stuck-up for 'space'.

'Think of me as your man Stephen Hawkings with better glasses and a sexier phone manner.'

Rory was dead keen on space when he was little. He wanted to be an astronaut. Before that he wanted to be a roadmender with a little stripy tent, and before that he wanted to be a pantomime horse. Now I understand he was just trying to get to share a confined space with another man. I've seen the size of his and Dino's flat and he's living the feckin' dream there, I tell you. Swing a cat? You couldn't even swing a passport photo of cat in there without having an eye out.

Anyway, Rory taught me all about space from the books he got from the library, so I'm basically pretty clued up on this. Think of me as your man Stephen Hawkings with better glasses and a sexier phone manner.

so·nar [soh-nahr]
noun: from the Roman word 'sonarus', meaning 'sonar', which is stuck-up for 'space'.

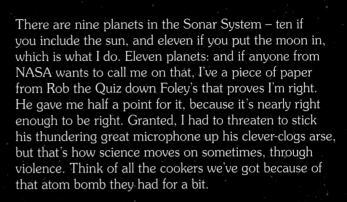

There are nine planets in the Sonar System – ten if you include the sun, and eleven if you put the moon in, which is what I do. Eleven planets: and if anyone from NASA wants to call me on that, I've a piece of paper from Rob the Quiz down Foley's that proves I'm right. He gave me half a point for it, because it's nearly right enough to be right. Granted, I had to threaten to stick his thundering great microphone up his clever-clogs arse, but that's how science moves on sometimes, through violence. Think of all the cookers we've got because of that atom bomb they had for a bit.

I wouldn't trust NASA's astrologers anyway – what do they know? They changed their mind about Pluto being a planet a few years back. Pluto? Not a planet? My arse. What else is it? Feckin' great thing spinning round in space? A lampshade? One of them balls they have on the ceiling at the dinner dance? Make up your feckin' mind, Alfred Einstein. You'll be telling me a tomato is a fruit next. (And don't start that again. It's not a fruit, or you wouldn't be able to put it in a salad. I mean, whoever heard of a fruit salad? Ludicrous.)

I find the best way to explain the planets is with chocolates. That way, you can eat your science afterwards, which you can't do with that experiment with all the blue crystals in a cup Cathy brought back from school once for homework. Jaysus, but Grandad was sicking up smurf juice for days.

SUN
Minstrel

Only the melt-proof Minstrel will do here, because the planet the Sun is not only the biggest planet in the Sonar System, it's also the hottest. It won't stop burning. It's worse than when a chip pan goes up. All life on Earth depends on the Sun, apparently, from elephants (important) to wasps (not fussed). We've only got to worry if some terrorist sends a big wet tea towel into space. Now, that'd be a great film right there. (Idea copyright Agnes Brown, usual fees.)

VENUS
Caramel Heart

Planet of love. Venus is famous for being the planet of the Sonar System that Winnie's cousin Bridget claims she was abducted by these tall orange fellas from. They took her aboard their spaceship, apparently, and interrogated her by probing her up the arse. Feck alone knows what they were hoping to find up there, but they'd get more sense out of that end than the one with the mouth on it. She's never been the same since she was kicked by that milk horse when she worked at Merville's.

MOON
Sucked Malteser

Crumbly, bumpy little planet the Moon is here played by the sucked Malteser. I think the dog had it. Or Grandad, when his teeth were out. Of all the planets that man has never landed on, the Moon is the most well known, because it's the only one you can see from the garden. The moon changes shape because of how cheese heats up in the sun, and these moon-changes affect life on Earth, causing tides, mood swings and that weird fur that grows on fondant fancies if you leave them in a Tupperware box too long.

MERCURY
Brazilian Darkness

Dark chocolate for this planet of mystery, with bits of nut in it that get between your teeth, like I imagine the planet would if you tried to eat it. Mercury is littlest of all the planets, but I couldn't find a small chocolate – apart from those drops the dog has – and I'm not having those chocolate raisins in the house after Grandad ate that big bag. You might as well eat rabbit shit. They go in the same way they feckin' come out, and that's never a good sign.

EARTH
Golden Barrel

The best chocolate for the best planet. If you want to know more about Planet Earth, please refer to the book in your hand, which contains all available current knowledge on the subject. Especially the important stuff (see Laundry).

MARS
Mars Planet

Mars, the red planet, used to be played by the strawberry fondant creme in my chocolate Sonar System, but I spotted these down Londis and I couldn't believe it! A chocolate called a Mars Planet! And my horoscope that morning had said I'd receive a message from the universe that it was time to make a change! Sure, but science is a magical thing. Mars is the planet that has had the most songs written about it (after the planet the Moon and the planet the Sun), and these songs include that Elton John one about the rocket and I'm sure Daniel Bowie did one, and it must turn up in that Chris de Burgh Christmas song 'A Snowman Came Travelling', and if it doesn't, he missed a trick because, as this list proves, Mars is without question the planet of song.

SATURN
Hazel Whirl

The cardboard bit on this Hazel Whirl represents the majestic 'Wings of Saturn', which are the most beautiful things in the Sonar System, apart from the face a newborn baby pulls when it's filling its little nappy, bless it.

URANUS
Ferrari Rocher

They'll not be making this one 'not a planet', but if they do, they'd better replace it with one with a name that's just as good: 'Feckelpus' or 'Testiculus Major' or 'Yourbum'. There's precious little humour in the galaxy these days, and didn't they go buggering a load of perfectly good Mickey Mouse jokes when they hoicked Pluto into the bin? Feckin' scientists. Too busy staring at the vast infinity of space to get the bigger picture.

JUPITER
Lindt Chocolate

The king of planets deserves the poshest chocolate: the Lindt. It might have a funny name, but it's feckin' lush. A Rolls-Royce in chocolate. Jupiter is the largest of the planets except the planet the Sun, but if you picked it up, it would weigh less than this chocolate, and that's because it's made of farts. And why it's made of farts is one of the mysteries of the universe. What's down there, in the middle of this planet of guffs? And what's it been eating? Maybe we'll never know. (Probably casserole, or that primordial soup I'm always reading about – though I've yet to find a feckin' recipe for it, which doesn't seem right for something so popular.)

PLUTO
Fruit Pastille

Because this is no longer a planet, apparently. Jaysus. I know what's going on here, boffins, you can't fool me. It's the furthest one away, and they can't be bothered to go there or look at it properly, so they start pretending it's none of their business, the lazy gobshites. Just like Hilliary does with that bit at the end of her garden she's 'leaving wild'. She's never feckin' been down there. And she won't pay the poor fella who does her garden to go and tidy it up, so she's hidden it all behind a bastard great hedge. No. Pluto *is* a planet. It's *your* job. Find out about it. Earn your money. Egghead feckers.

THE OTHER ONE
Country Fudge

Hard to remember what this one's called or where it goes. Can't wait for this one to not be a planet any more.

If you want to remember the order of the planets, I use this simple trick:

'Peter Piper Picked a Peck of Pickled Pepper Pecause Peter Piper's a Pucking Numpty'.

Which stands for:

> Planet the Sun
> Planet Mercury
> Planet Venus
> Planet Earth
> Planet the Moon
> Planet Mars
> Planet Jupiter
> Planet Saturn
> Planet The Other One
> Planet Uranus
> Not a planet Pluto

When Pluto used to be planet (which it still is), the phrase used to end with Peter Piper being a Pucking Prick. If you ask me, he was. Why anyone'd steal pepper, let alone pickled pepper, is a total mystery to me. He was probably a heavy smoker and needed to go some to get his taste buds to wake up. Redser was like that. Used to put curry powder in his mustard.

Pluto
Still a feckin' planet

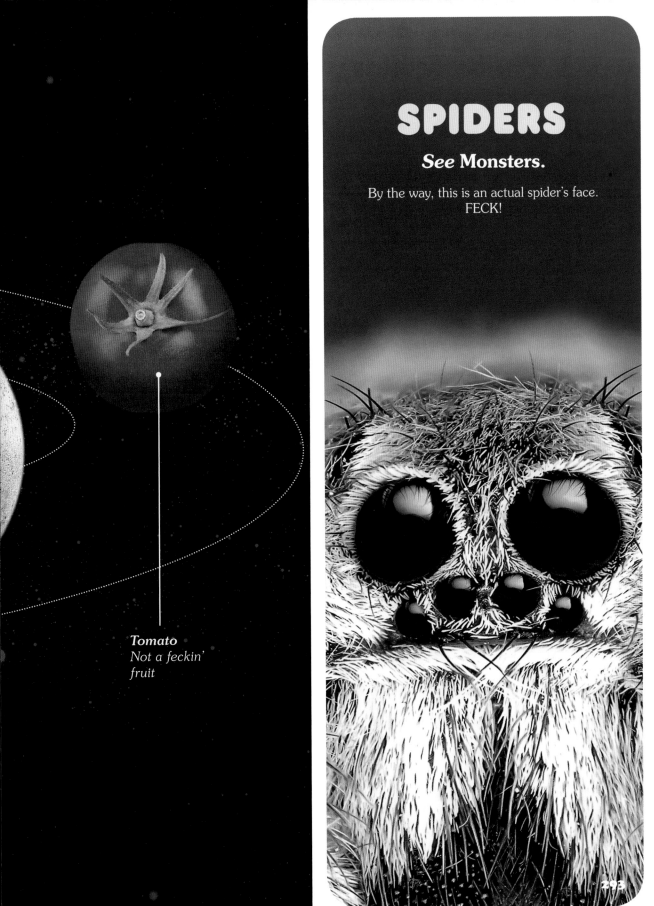

SPIDERS

See Monsters.

By the way, this is an actual spider's face.
FECK!

Tomato
*Not a feckin'
fruit*

SPORT

Sport is a way for men to spend as much time as possible away from their families without needing to be in prison. Some men like to play sport, but more of them like to watch it, because that way they don't have to put their drink down.

Sure, but that doesn't stop them pretending they're playing. Jaysus. The way they go on about the game, you'd think they were right there in the middle of the action rather than pressing a dent in the sofa like you'd used it to store a couple of heavy watermelons.

And it's all We, We, We. A man watching the football puts more We's in the wrong place than he does in the gents in Foley's at closing time. 'We played a good game.' 'We thrashed you lot.' 'Sure, We were robbed there.' No, you weren't. You were at home on your feckin' arse. Someone else was playing. Someone half your feckin' age, who doesn't grunt like a stuck boar when they move from a sitting to a standing position.

Some people say sport is a religion. It's certainly full of a lot of shite that makes no feckin' sense. Men get fearsome superstitious about it.

Try and get a man to miss watching a game because you want him to do something else, something he doesn't consider as important, like fixing the guttering or attending his own daughter's wedding. Or attending his own wedding.

No. They won't budge, they've got to watch every feckin' game, just in case. Just in case what? No feckin' idea. It's as if they're worried the players check before they go to kick the ball, and if himself on the sofa has popped to the feckin' toilet, they'll sky the feckin' thing on purpose, to teach him a lesson for losing focus.

What are they waiting for? Do they think if a player breaks his ankle, the manager's going to come running on to the pitch shouting, 'Is there anyone watching at home who can step in? We're changing our formation and the coach is looking for a balding man in his early 50s with a bent back and sky-high cholesterol and last season's away shirt covered in Wotsit dust and flecks of creosote…If you fit this description, catch the next available bus! Save us! You're our only hope!'

I wouldn't mind if they looked like they were enjoying all the supporting. But they make it look such hard feckin' work. When their bunch of lads loses, they don't want to talk about it. And when they win, you can't talk to them, because they're drunk. It's like living with a manic-depressive Trappist monk who's siphoning beer out the monastery barrels.

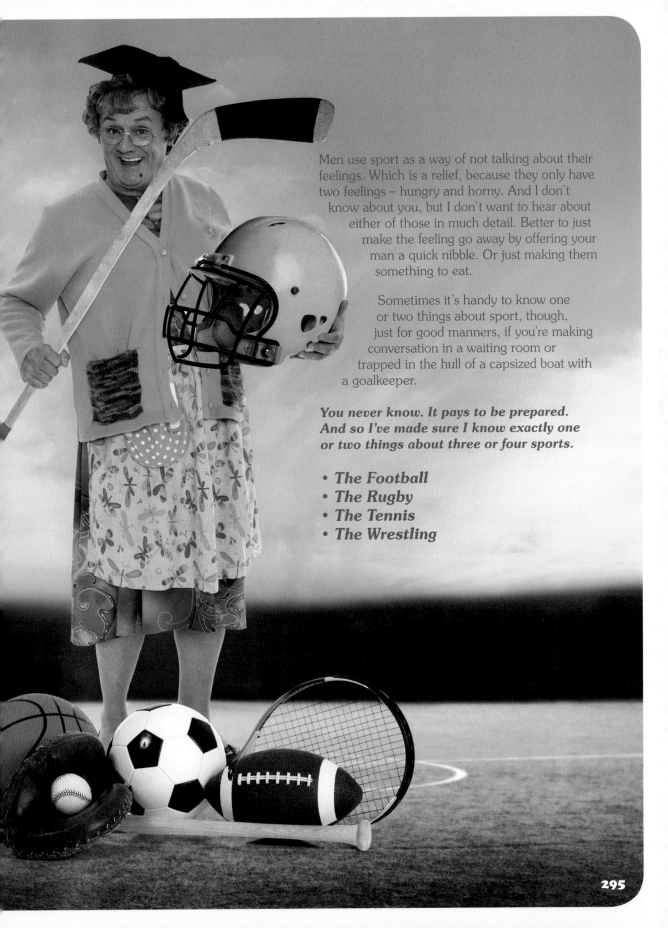

Men use sport as a way of not talking about their feelings. Which is a relief, because they only have two feelings – hungry and horny. And I don't know about you, but I don't want to hear about either of those in much detail. Better to just make the feeling go away by offering your man a quick nibble. Or just making them something to eat.

Sometimes it's handy to know one or two things about sport, though, just for good manners, if you're making conversation in a waiting room or trapped in the hull of a capsized boat with a goalkeeper.

You never know. It pays to be prepared. And so I've made sure I know exactly one or two things about three or four sports.

- *The Football*
- *The Rugby*
- *The Tennis*
- *The Wrestling*

THE FOOTBALL

Offside

You need to know the offside rule. It's not hard: the offside rule is that if a man is explaining the offside rule to you, and another man is between you and the first man, but not actively already in play, the second man is declared to be in an 'offside' position in the conversation, and may insist that the first man has forgotten some important part of the offside rule.

He may then start explaining the offside rule to you as well, by which time both of them will have missed whatever bollocks was happening on the television and get cross with each other, and you can slip past them both into the kitchen for a nice cup of tea.

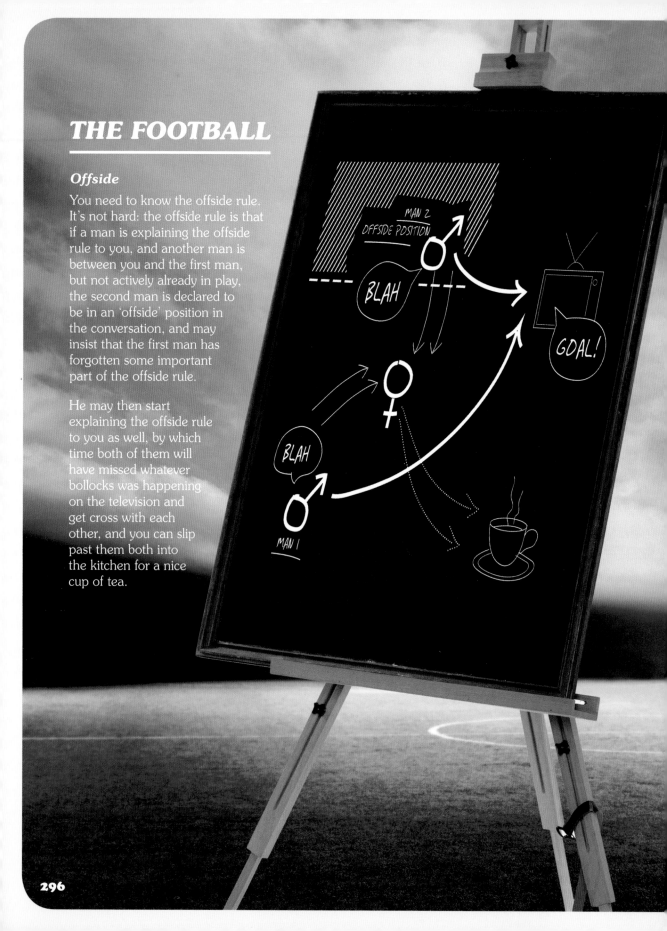

Costumes

Every team has two costumes: one for playing on their own pitch, one for playing on someone else's. They're different colours, so they don't get confused with the team they're playing against. Except sometimes both teams end up with the same colours. Then they go back to wearing the first colour. Or rather, only one of them does. I'm not sure which one. I'm not at all sure how this works. I thought I knew this one. Anyway, you need to buy both yourself, plus a scarf for pulling the nippers along in a cart. The football stadium's far too far to expect them to walk.

Referees

You can learn a lot about The Football from listening to the stuff that's shouted in the front room, and one interesting fact I've picked up is that all referees suffer from terrible bad eyesight caused by masturbating, which I think they do to cheer themselves up after being born the wrong side of the bed sheets.

Fig. 1
Wonky ball
made by an
eejit so you
can't kick it

Fig. 2
Big lads

THE RUGBY

Wonky Balls

The Rugby is like The Football but for people who think that the beautiful game is too easy. So the ball's been made by an eejit, so you can't kick it, which makes the game too hard. So the rugby lads are allowed to pick it up and just take it to the goal, which makes the game too easy. So they're allowed to punch the living daylights out of the one with the ball, which makes the game too hard again. So he's allowed to throw the ball, which makes the game too easy. So he's not allowed to throw the ball anywhere useful, which makes the game too hard. And that's rugby.

Big Lads

I tell you who's a great ambassador for the game of The Rugby. Whoever it was who kept taking his shirt off on *Strictly Come Dancing*. There might have been two of them. I lose track. But they really made the sport come alive. Or were they rowers?

THE SKIING

Ski? Load of bollix.
Unless it's the yoghurty kind.

THE TENNIS

Bedroom Noises

The Tennis is very popular these days, and I'll tell you for why. Men. Watching the women get all exerted. Jaysus, it's the same as ever it was. And now the women make the most disgraceful noises, like wild animals. If I lived downstairs from Centre Court at Wimbledon, I'd be banging on the ceiling with a broom. If I wanted to hear that sort of panting and grunting, I'd stand outside Dermot's room when he borrows Cathy's laptop. It gives the crowd quite the wrong idea.

And the skirts. Well, we know what all the men at home are thinking of. They're thinking of that poster with the girl playing tennis with the itchy arse. That's what they're thinking of. It's not sport. It's filth in rubber-soled shoes, that's what it is.

Cavity wall insulation

Fig. 3
Filth in rubber-soled shoes

302

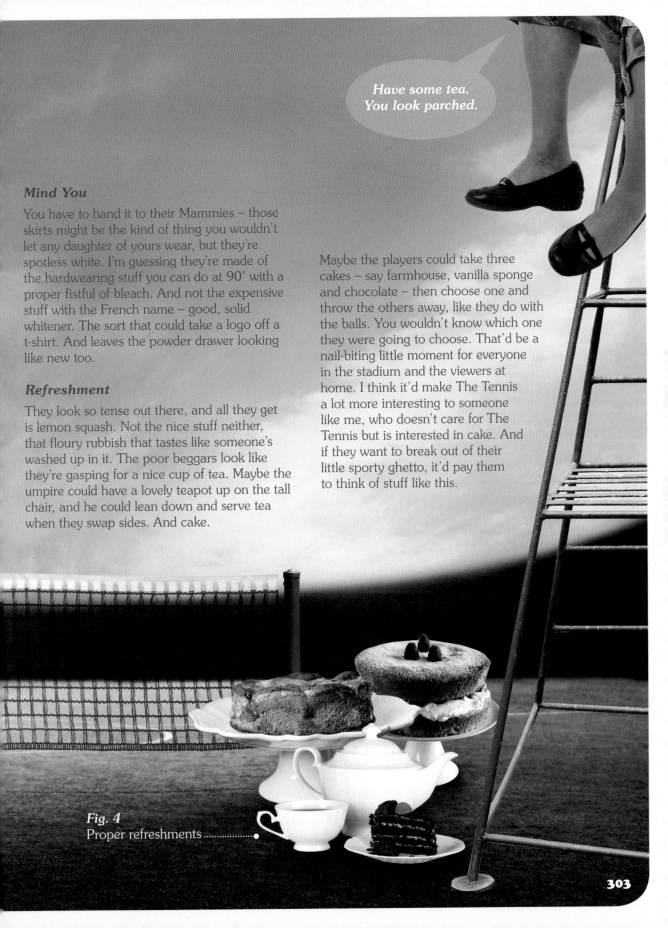

*Have some tea.
You look parched.*

Mind You

You have to hand it to their Mammies – those skirts might be the kind of thing you wouldn't let any daughter of yours wear, but they're spotless white. I'm guessing they're made of the hardwearing stuff you can do at 90° with a proper fistful of bleach. And not the expensive stuff with the French name – good, solid whitener. The sort that could take a logo off a t-shirt. And leaves the powder drawer looking like new too.

Refreshment

They look so tense out there, and all they get is lemon squash. Not the nice stuff neither, that floury rubbish that tastes like someone's washed up in it. The poor beggars look like they're gasping for a nice cup of tea. Maybe the umpire could have a lovely teapot up on the tall chair, and he could lean down and serve tea when they swap sides. And cake.

Maybe the players could take three cakes – say farmhouse, vanilla sponge and chocolate – then choose one and throw the others away, like they do with the balls. You wouldn't know which one they were going to choose. That'd be a nail-biting little moment for everyone in the stadium and the viewers at home. I think it'd make The Tennis a lot more interesting to someone like me, who doesn't care for The Tennis but is interested in cake. And if they want to break out of their little sporty ghetto, it'd pay them to think of stuff like this.

Fig. 4
Proper refreshments.................

THE WRESTLING

My kind of sport.

Honest, man-to-man throwing around. And even more enjoyable when it's in a ring with fancy clothes and not just two drunken yellow-eyed sacks clearing the floor at the pub.

Anyone who thinks The Wrestling
is rigged ought to have seen
some of the scraps I've witnessed.
Wattie Whelan was the crowned
champion of pub wrestling. He could
take a chair to the head and not even
blink. (I put this down to his reactions
being too slow.) I once saw him get
a man in a headlock and fall asleep.
And even then the poor fella couldn't
shake Wattie off.

Fig. 5
Fancy-dressed
Honest
Manly

SUITCASE CONTAINING ALL THE IMPORTANT STUFF, THE

Under every Mammy's bed is a suitcase that, like her husband, has definitely seen better days, is a bit more faded and wrinkly than it used to be, is stiffer and heavier than you expect. And smells a bit musty by now. And is full of shit.

Mind you, it's the important shit you keep in this bit of unwanted baggage. Here, if you need to lay hands on it in a hurry, is where you'll find:

• **Mammy's will.**

• **Mammy's life insurance paperwork.**

• **Mammy's savings account book** that hasn't been updated since 1969, with all the entries handwritten and in punts and pence. Liquidate that goldmine and you'd have enough in your hand to buy you half a pint at Foley's, with enough change to not buy another one. When that cash was first paid in, you could have bought the entire bucking pub with it. That's inflatulence for you.

• **Love letters from Mammy's youth.**
Not as interesting as you'd think. A fella never wrote down anything too racy in those days, in case his Mam saw. He just whispered it to you in the back row of the Adelphi, usually during the newsreel so it seemed even filthier. 'Suggesting that sort of thing in front of visiting dignitaries? Outrageous. You deserve a slap.' (That kind of talk only encouraged them. And that's why I did it.)

• **The only thing Mammy has ever won.**
Might be a swimming badge, might be a baking certificate. Mine's a bottle of throat spray I won in a church raffle in 1957. It might be out of date by now, for all I know. I'll get Grandad to try it.

SAVINGS BOOK

NAME Agnes Brown
Life Savings

'The suitcase is like a husband ... it has definitely seen better days, is a bit more faded and wrinkly than it used to be, is stiffer and heavier than you expect. And smells a bit musty by now. And is full of shit.'

Fig. 1
One for every boiler
I've ever had

• **Congratulations cards and telegrams from every time Mammy had a baby.** Jaysus, I've such a haul of these I had to find a second suitcase. I've had so many nippers I don't even remember some of the ones I'm being congratulated on having. I'm sure I never had a Padraig or a Spike. Come to think of it, maybe there were some other Mammy's cards in the case when I picked it up from the jumble. Probably best not to throw them out in case one of mine turns up who I've forgotten emigrated and they take offence.

• **An unidentified trinket.** Put there especially to torture Mammy's memory in later years. 'Sure, what is this? Is it a pill box? A knob from me first record player? Something that fell off a posh shoe?' Pretty and useless. Like one of those Kardashian creatures, but in dusty Bakelite.

• **A few tattered photos that Mammy's Mammy gave her of her Mammy,** probably with another Mammy's Mammy's Mammy. Or something like that. Unless someone thought to write down who they were on the back, it might as well be the cover of a book of heartfelt memoirs with a title like *I Remember Balaghaderreen* or *Tears in Tobercurry* or *An Ummerantarry Bog Childhood*. Or *The Complete History*

of Laundry, if they're in pinafores and their publishers have got any feckin' sense. Anyway, it's a photo you'd feel terrible about throwing away, even though you've no feckin' idea who these two strangers are from Adam. That's family for you. Loyalty, even when there's no point. Like with Grandad.

• **Boiler manuals.** I don't know anyone in my family who's ever tried to repair the boiler since Redser lost his eyebrows that time. You get a man in. But every boiler we've ever had is commemorated in The Suitcase.

Fig. 2
Mammy or is it
Mammy's Mammy?

SWEARING

Even when you're up for the hundredth night in a row with your tit in what seems like the hundredth hungry chiseller in a row, a Mammy knows that her little angels aren't going to stay babbies forever.

From the moment they come out of you screaming and wailing – and them making a noise almost as bad – they're moving away from you. They're growing up and moving into the world. And that's your responsibility. You can't cross your fingers and hope they can make do with what they get told in the playground. They need to learn it, and they need to learn it from you. It may seem rude, but they need to know the Facts of Life.

I'm talking about swearing.

There are certain things a parent must pass on to a child: a sense of right and wrong, a collection of artist-crafted heirloom collectable figurines that are going to be worth a fortune one day you wait and see, and a proper grounding in how to swear.

The nippers don't always know what's rude. But they pick up all sorts from their parents. Sure, I remember when Mark was about five, he went on a school trip to the zoo. At the end of the day, his teacher (sour-faced old bat, she was) handed him back to me, saying, **'Mrs Brown – I don't know what your Mark hears at home, but we don't want to hear it at St Saviour's.'** I didn't know what she was on about. I thought he'd been singing Russ Conway or something.

So I asked him.

Poor little thing, he was devastated. He said, 'Mammy, I said a bad word today.'

And I said, 'Oh, did you?'

And he said, 'I did, Mammy.'

So I asked him why. And he looked up at me and said, 'I didn't know what else to say.'

And I said, 'Sure, Mark, you know you're meant to keep bad words inside you and not let them out.'

And he said again, 'But I couldn't think what else to say.'

So I said, 'Well, what was it? It can't have been that bad.'

(I thought, the poor little blighter's said 'shut up' to someone and upset that rotten teacher of his.)

And he said, 'I was looking at the fish, Mammy. And they were so lovely – some of them were orange, and some had bright-blue stripes that looked like the thing on the wall of the chipper that kills flies, and they were so amazing…'

'Mrs Flaherty! ...Look at these f*ckin' fish!'

So I said, 'Then what bad word did you say?'

He blushed.

And he told me. 'I said to the teacher, "Mrs Flaherty! Look at these fuckin' fish!"'

Now then. I know what you're thinking: a five-year-old using language like that. Disgraceful.

But you know what I was thinking?

I was thinking: THAT'S MY BOY.

Because he'd learned the first rule of swearing, and that's *make it fuckin' count.*

If you're going to swear, you've got to do it properly. And that means landing one on your audience. And by hell he landed one on Mrs Flaherty. (And by the looks of the back of his legs, she landed a couple on him too. Miserable old cow.)

So I went up the school the next day, and I found Sourbag Flaherty and cornered her. And I said, 'Our Mark says he had a lovely day at the zoo yesterday. But I think he must have got bitten by something, because he's got two great smarts on his legs. Have you any idea what might have bitten him?' And she blushed a bit and said, 'I don't know, Mrs Brown. Maybe it was an insect. Sometimes where there's still water you get mosquitoes.'

And I said, 'Ah, that'll be it. Not to worry. I'll put some vinegar on it.' And I walked away and Mrs Flaherty relaxed a bit. 'Tell you what, though,' I said to her, 'must have been a pretty big mosquito. Good job I wasn't there. I'd have flattened the fucker.' She got the point.

The Fecks of Life, Or,
How to Teach the Littluns to Swear

Start them out with something simple, like
'gobshite'. You'd be amazed how many nursery
rhymes it fits into. Like:

**Gobshite, gobshite, have you any wool?
Yes sir, yes sir, three bags full.**

Or:

**Gobshite, gobshite, little star,
How I wonder what you are.**

And they're all to the same feckin' tune, so you
might as well add:

**Gobshite, gobshite, E, F, G,
H, I, J, K, L-M-N-O-P.**

Gobshite, gobshite, have you any wool?

Gobshite, gobshite, little star

by Agnes Brown

Although that one can mess up their understanding of the alphabet. So best not. You can even write up some flashcards, with easy-to-read things like 'sod' or 'bollix' on them. Make sure you spell them right, mind.

Once you've got their foul-mouthed feet under the table, reach for something more ambitious, like 'twat' or 'dickhead'. Now they're well on their way. And they've got some useful ammo. (Anything that calls someone an idiot is useful ammo.)

Whatever you do, *don't teach them pretend swearing*. Pretend swearing is the feckin' worst.

There was a lad on our street – very strict parents (they made him eat his food in alphabetical order) – who used to say, 'Oh my hat!' Poor fella. He might as well have gone round with 'kick my fluffy arse' written on the back of his jacket. No one ever took him seriously. He ended up being Dublin's first bingo-calling priest. Father Fingal O'Dingal. (To be fair, no one took him seriously from the day the maternity nurse wrote his name on the wrist-tag.)

When the nippers are a bit older, you can start them on the hard stuff: 'bloody', 'bastard', 'fanny','cock in a frock', that sort of thing. And once you've given them the proper vocabulary, you need to teach them the main thing about swearing: time and place. What to say, when and where to say it.

Degrees of Swearing

You need to know what's right for the situation.

So, if you hit your thumb with a hammer, 'Damn and blast!' isn't enough, and 'Fuck a priest!' is too much. You want to aim for something on the lower end of the scale, something that gives everyone an idea of how much pain you're in but that doesn't make it sound like you've got the business end of a rifle up your arse. I recommend something like **'Christ in shitty nappies!'** That'll do the trick.

On the other hand, if some gobshite nearly runs you down at a zebra crossing, that's the time to pull out the big guns. That's when 'Silly arse!' isn't enough and 'Your mother sucks cocks in Argos!' is (only slightly) too much. Something like a simple 'Fuck' between punches is perfect.

There's many a fuck-up in a pair of hot knackers!

Then there's the socially awkward situation, like someone announcing a pregnancy out of wedlock. This one you have to play carefully. 'God's walnuts!' isn't enough and 'Shit me a prisoner!' seems wrong. Something like **'There's many a fuck-up in a pair of hot knackers!'** is about right. But you have to say it like you're concerned, not like you hope to find the poor girl selling her few bits of furniture for IOUs in two years' time.

Remember rule number one: swearing should be fun. Not cruel. Just telling someone to eff off is no fun. You've got to tell them to fuck themselves backwards into a room full of celibates. (And even then, that doesn't make any sense.)

Christ in shitty nappies!

MAMMY'S SWEAR CHART

I do all my swearing by a strict chart of strength, like they have for storms at sea.

WORD	LOW STRENGTH	FULL FAT
ARSE	Bum Bumholes	Arse Arseaches Arsewits Arseholes Arsemurder
BOLLIX	Balls Ballses Bollixes	Bollix Bollixfaces Christ's fizzy bollix on the cross
SHIT	Scheisse (it's foreign) Shite Shitsies	Shit Shitsticks Shitshitshitshitshit
FUCK	Buck Feck	Fuck Fuckaroo Fuckarooney Fuckarama Fuck-knuckles Fuckshitarsemurder

FULL-FAT
SELECTION

BOLLIXFACES

FUCK-KNUCKLES

CHRIST'S FIZZY BOLLIX ON THE CROSS

FUCKAROONEY

IS FOR...

TEETH

You've got to look after your teeth, my Auntie Frances told me. That was easy for her to say: she kept hers in a cup next to her Danielle Steel and only put them in for lamb. They got less use than Kojak's comb.

But I've always cleaned my teeth morning and night, and after meals (except when I can't be arsed, when I've found a Polo has roughly the same effect). And I've still got all my own teeth. They're in a drawer in an old Euthymol tin. I saved them up because Micky Hagan told me in the playground that the Tooth Fairy paid extra for bulk.

TEETHING is horrible painful for babbies. They make a right noise about it and you can't calm them down, which means you get no sleep at all. I used to keep a bottle of brandy handy (we all did back then), but I found it gave me such a fierce hangover in the morning I might as well have stayed up and looked after the babby.

Children get a set of teeth, then they lose them almost as soon as they've got them, usually just before a school photograph, so they can have a lovely boxer's smile. I think that's evidence that God had a bad night's sleep before thinking up teeth. The maths is all wrong. Look:

Milk teeth 1 year–approx. 10 years old

Adult teeth Approx. 10 years old–death

Diagram 1. The two phases of teeth

A whole set of teeth for ten years. And then another set that's meant to last you for a lifetime's chewing. I know you do most of your serious gobstopper and toffee work in those first ten years, and the wiser head opts for soft centres and suckables as the years go by, but those first teeth have a feckin' easy ride. You could keep them for another decade or so and make them do their fair share.

I think it's evidence that we're meant to die at about 25, like everyone did in the olden days, because of working hard in the fields and plough accidents and sabre-toothed tigers. We're living way longer than our teeth were designed for. And what are scientists working on? Bagless vacuum cleaners. I want a third set of teeth. Or a new set every ten years. And proper ones, that grow, not ones I have to get from the dentist.

Is that too much to ask?

If it's not, I'll have a set of wings as well. And knees that wake up before I do, unlike this useless pair I've got now, which have a couple of hours' lie-in every feckin' day, even when the rest of me is up and about.

TELEVISION

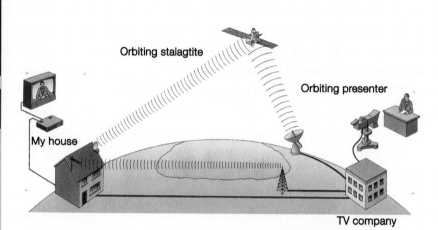

Orbiting stalagtite

Orbiting presenter

My house

TV company

In Brief

Television might seem like impossible magic, but I found a picture and it looks like it's quite simple. Here's how it definitely works:

1. Viewer looks for remote control*
2. Finds it under Grandad*
3. Gets laundry tongs from kitchen (see Laundry)*
4. Retrieves remote control with tongs*
5. Using remote control, pushes button which asks for programme*
6. Request travels up wires to TV company (see picture)
7. TV company tells orbiting TV presenter to make programme
8. Orbiting presenter sends programme to nearby stalagtite
9. Stalagtite drops programme on to viewer's roof

*Not shown

27th *This week*

I'm not sure why the presenter has to be in orbit. It's probably something to do with that Orzone layer they used to have before Cathy made me change deodorant. (I still use the hairspray, mind. Until they invent roll-on hairspray, I don't have much of a choice.)

And what the feck happened to remote controls? They used to be a doodad the size of a chocolate bar with four numbers, a thing for volume and a big red knob. Now they look like the flight deck of a feckin' 747. I babysat Bono once and couldn't get Mark and

Betty's telly to do anything. Turned out the gogglebox worked off the thing on the side table I thought was a new electronic piano, and the little whatnot whose button I'd been mashing had been flipping their garage door open and shut all night. Him and her came home to find a burglar had been bashed unconscious trying to make off with their Flymo.

Plenty of people don't know how to set up their television set, but it's important to have your television adjusted correctly, and that depends on your age.

What's happening on the square?

EastEnders p. 33

What's happening in the circle?

p. 15

Age `0–10`

Colours up full, volume high, for simple undemanding programmes with people falling over in them and lots of songs.

Age `11–20`

On in the background, while doing something more interesting. Like having a picture in the fireplace of people taking paternity tests.

Age `21–40`

Normal volume. Normal colours. It's all you do in the evening because you're knackered and you've got two hours between putting the kids down and collapsing in a heap. You might have to turn it up if you're eating something noisy, like pork scratchings.

Age `40–55`

Off most of the time. Harder to find anything you want to watch, and volume high because you can't hear what anyone's feckin' saying. Jaysus, does everyone do mumbling at drama school these days? Whatever happened to SPEAKING CLEARLY?

Age `55–65`

On most of the time. Mainly gardening programmes, repeats and old detective shows. No longer bothered what anyone's saying. It's just a comfort to have some noise in the room now neither of you have a word to say to each other.

Age `65+`

Colours up full, volume high, for simple undemanding programmes with people falling over in them and lots of songs.

THAT WOMAN

That Woman. You know the one. Every family has a That Woman.

That Woman is the one who's known as That Woman. Not by her name.

That Woman is the one with the face like a cat's arse. Puckered. And a bit furry.

That Woman is the one who tells you about all the successful friends she's got, even though you never see her with them.

She's the one who puts on make-up to go to the feckin' jumble sale. And buys nothing.

She's the one who asks if you've got a fancy drink when you offer her a sherry. 'Do you have a Martini, darling?' 'No, but I've got a Mantovani LP in the loft if you fancy climbing the ladder.'

She's the one you cut out of the wedding photos. Eventually. Even if you have to stick the two halves back together and someone loses an arm. It's a small price to pay.

She's the one you give one of those tiny Christmas cards to – the ones about the size of a stamp that say, 'This cost feck all and I wish I hadn't spent nearly that much.'

She's the one who always looks like she's ready to leave. And then stays till the bitter feckin' end.

She's the one who invites you over to her place 'for drinks and canopies' (no idea what that means, but I've been to loads of these godforsaken shindigs and never seen so much as an awning) and then serves teeny tiny miniature burgers, as if she wants everyone in the room to feel like giants. (Last time I went to Hilliary's, she handed round these weird little pancakes covered in what looked like greasy full stops that tasted like Maggi. I told her it looked like her typewriter had been sick.)

She's the one who you can hear coming because her wrists are covered in feckin' bangles that jingle and jangle like a rag-and-bone man with a truck full of old clocks.

She's the one with a brand-new shopping bag that says 'Love Me, I'm Reusable' on it. (Isn't it funny how you never see that on other reusable things, like doors and pants?)

She's the one who has 'real' versions of things. A real fire. Real pasta. A real Christmas tree. Real tomatoes. (Like there are pretend tomatoes. Little sour bastards hiding in the salad that turn out to be Russian spies.)

She's the one who spends hours painting old furniture so it looks even older.

That Woman. Fuck her.

If there's one thing I've learned, it's how to play the mouth organ. And if there's two things I've learned, it's how to play the mouth organ and that nobody can leave a feckin' thermostat alone.

+ +

I have the thermostat at home set at a constant comfortable 23 degrees, not so cold that I can see my breath, not so hot that I stick to the vinyl seats at the kitchen table so when I stand up it makes a noise like an octopus releasing a submarine.

But nobody will leave the fecker alone. Every time I check it, someone's fiddled with it. They deny it, but I've rumbled them all at it. I'm like the Columbo of Finglas. I know who's tweaked it, and I'm prepared to dust for fingerprints, turn a chair round (not one of the vinyl ones, in case of the noise) and play bad cop.

Redser used to turn the 'stat down to almost nothing. Freezing, he'd have it. Some days I'd warm myself up by standing in front of the fridge and opening the little door where the fish fingers live.

He'd say he couldn't feel the cold, but he could feel the wind blowing round his wallet where the money used to be, the feckin' cheapskate. Standing in the kitchen in a duffel coat and balaclava like Ranulph Twistleton Thungummybob, asking what the problem was, frost on his eyelashes and nuts like little frozen peas.

After he'd passed, God rest him, I'd keep finding the thermostat turned down, and for a while I took it as a sign that he was still around, still following me around the house, still being a pain in the feckin' arse. But I found out it was Rory. He hates the warm because he doesn't like his cheeks being pink. No problem with every other thing he feckin' owns being pink, but who am I to judge?

Dermot, on the other hand, is always turning the feckin' thermostat up. It's like keeping a tropical pet. I think he likes it warm so he can doze off more easily. And Cathy's no better. I said if she wore a cardigan, buttoned up properly, she wouldn't feel it, but she's always blaming her circulation. She wants to worry a bit less about the blood pumping round her feet and more about the hot water pumping round my feckin' radiators. Redser may have gone, but so's his money, and a woman can't go spending on central heating when there's drawers full of unworn wool will do the job for a fraction of the cost.

Anyway, I always take a photo of my thermostat, every day, so I know where I've left it. That way I can prove someone's been tampering with the settings. And I get them printed out at Fastprint down the arcade, and I bind them into a book.

And if you ever, ever get on my nerves showing me pictures of your nieces in feckin' mortarboards and what they've done to the pool tiling on your holiday home in the Costa del Pissoff, Hilliary Nicolson, I am perfectly prepared to get out my thermostat album and talk you through every one of those feckin' photos, blow-by-blow. You see if I don't.

The
Thermostat Album

WARNING: MAY CAUSE STATIC SHOCK

Thunder Sheets

SHOCK ABSORBANT

150 SQ FT (13.93 m²),
300 2-PLY SHEETS PER ROLL,
4.5 IN x 4.0 IN (11.43 cm x 10.16 cm)

4 DOUBLE ROLLS

ring blanket

TOG RATING
○○○○○

150 SQ FT (13.93 m²),
300 2-PLY SHEETS PER ROLL,
4.5 IN x 4.0 IN (11.43 cm x 10.16 cm)

4 DOUBLE ROLLS

Bog Ribbon

150 SQ FT (13.93 m²),
300 2-PLY SHEETS PER ROLL,
4.5 IN x 4.0 IN (11.43 cm x 10.16 cm)

4 DOUBLE ROLLS

PUPPY'S
SCARVES

150 SQ FT (13.93 m²),
300 2-PLY SHEETS PER ROLL,
4.5 IN x 4.0 IN (11.43 cm x 10.16 cm)

10P

crease-proof paper

EXTRA CRUNCHY

150 SQ FT (13.93 m²),
300 2-PLY SHEETS PER ROLL,
4.5 IN x 4.0 IN (11.43 cm x 10.16 cm)

4 DOUBLE ROLLS

BACK-DOORMATS

BACK ENTRANCE EXCELLENCE

150 SQ FT (13.93 m²),
300 2-PLY SHEETS PER ROLL,
4.5 IN x 4.0 IN (11.43 cm x 10.16 cm)

4 DOUBLE ROLLS

DITCHCLOTHS

150 SQ FT (13.93 m²),
300 2-PLY SHEETS PER ROLL,
4.5 IN x 4.0 IN (11.43 cm x 10.16 cm)

4 DOUBLE ROLLS

bathroom
receipts

For when you nee

150 SQ FT (13.93 m²),
300 2-PLY SHEETS PER ROLL,
4.5 IN x 4.0 IN (11.43 cm x 10.16 cm)

Sausage Roll

150 SQ FT (13.93 m²),
300 2-PLY SHEETS PER ROLL,
4.5 IN x 4.0 IN (11.43 cm x 10.16 cm)

4 DOUBLE ROLLS

BROWNIE
PACKING

150 SQ FT (13.93 m²),
300 2-PLY SHEETS PER ROLL,
4.5 IN x 4.0 IN (11.43 cm x 10.16 cm)

4 DOUBLE ROLLS

CHOD WAD

150 SQ FT (13.93 m²),
300 2-PLY SHEETS PER ROLL,
4.5 IN x 4.0 IN (11.43 cm x 10.16 cm)

4 DOUBLE ROLLS

PANKE

150 SQ FT (13.93 m²),
300 2-PLY SHEETS PER ROLL,
4.5 IN x 4.0 IN (11.43 cm x 10.16 cm)

Tissue Pooper

150 SQ FT (13.93 m²),
300 2-PLY SHEETS PER ROLL,
4.5 IN x 4.0 IN (11.43 cm x 10.16 cm)

4 DOUBLE ROLLS

Eyepads

150 SQ FT (13.93 m²),
300 2-PLY SHEETS PER ROLL,
4.5 IN x 4.0 IN (11.43 cm x 10.16 cm)

4 DOUBLE ROLLS

Chutewipes

150 SQ FT (13.93 m²),
300 2-PLY SHEETS PER ROLL,
4.5 IN x 4.0 IN (11.43 cm x 10.16 cm)

4 DOUBLE ROLLS

150 SQ FT (13.93 m²),
300 2-PLY SHEETS PER ROLL,
4.5 IN x 4.0 IN (11.43 cm x 10.16 cm)

TOILET PAPER

There are some things in life a Mammy never scrimps on. Like bras. And teabags. And, above all, toilet paper.

Call it what you like!

BASICS
ARSEWIPE
DOES 2000 WIPES

150 SQ FT (13.93 m²),
300 2-PLY SHEETS PER ROLL,
4.5 IN x 4.0 IN (11.43 cm x 10.16 cm)

BUM BUNTING
TOILETTERIES ON A SHOESTRING

150 SQ FT (13.93 m²),
300 2-PLY SHEETS PER ROLL,
4.5 IN x 4.0 IN (11.43 cm x 10.16 cm)

TURD TOKENS

150 SQ FT (13.93 m²),
300 2-PLY SHEETS PER ROLL,
4.5 IN x 4.0 IN (11.43 cm x 10.16 cm)

CIGAR COUPONS

150 SQ FT (13.93 m²),
300 2-PLY SHEETS PER ROLL,
4.5 IN x 4.0 IN (11.43 cm x 10.16 cm)

Whatever you call it, you've got to buy the nice stuff.

Unless you like the feeling of giving your balloon knot a paper cut before rinsing it in battery acid and stumbling round for the rest of the day like someone trying to hold a goldfish bowl between their knees. Which I don't, and you shouldn't either, you filthy pervert.

It's this simple: you get what you feckin' pay for. And if you pay peanuts, you might as well wipe your arse with them for all the scratching and scraping. Plus – and every Mammy knows this – kiddies' fingers go through the cheap stuff. And once you've taken an old toothbrush to a nipper's stinky fingernails for the fourth or fifth time, you start to get the message.

I'm not talking about the triple-ply cushioned la-di-da stuff Hilliary gets. That's a waste of feckin' money right there. How much use do you get out of that, with every sheet the depth of an Axminster carpet? You'd do better unravelling a Swiss roll.

Grandad'd be calling down for me to bring him up a spare four-pack halfway through moving his roast of a Sunday night, and that's a sight you don't want to be forced to glimpse through the crack of the door.

Jaysus, I don't know if you've seen it, but there's this new thing doing the rounds: 'moist' toilet 'wipes'. Winnie swears by them. Says they leave your arse feeling like new (whatever that is). If you ask me, I don't want the word 'moist' anywhere near my bum. It's not right. 'Soft' is all right. So is 'strong'. 'Moist' just sounds like there's been an accident. 'Moist' is like a Christmas wreath: fine for the front entrance, wrong at the back.

Cathy looked it up on her computer, and it says toilet paper was invented by the Chinese. Just like televisions and t-shirts. They must be fierce busy, the Chinese, with all that making. It's no wonder they only have time for takeaways.

By the way, this isn't to be confused with '*the* toilet paper', the newspaper that men leave stuffed down the side of the lavvy. You know, the *Racing Post*, or an old copy of the *Metro Herald* folded over at the quizword. Redser used to spend more time hiding in the loo with a rag on his lap than he spent with the kids. And they're all the same. I'm surprised men don't get that Deep Pan Thrombosis.

Hilliary, I ask you, has books in hers. Books! On a feckin' shelf. 'Oh, I can't stop reading for a minute, me.' And not even proper ones like the one in your hands right now, designed by experts for enjoyment in the smallest room. Charles feckin' Dickens and *The Complete Works of Shakespeare*, for the love of feck. It's no wonder she needs the moist toilet paper. If she's crouching over the drop long enough to finish *Nicholas Copperfield*, her haemorrhoids must be something to behold. I imagine her knickers are like a bag of red-hot coals. Poor thing.

MADE IN CHINA

TOURISTS

Like visitors you haven't catered for. Whatever they ask for, point them at the docks. There's nothing you can't get down the docks (just ask Doctor Karoshi down the groin clinic), and they'll have a story to take home.

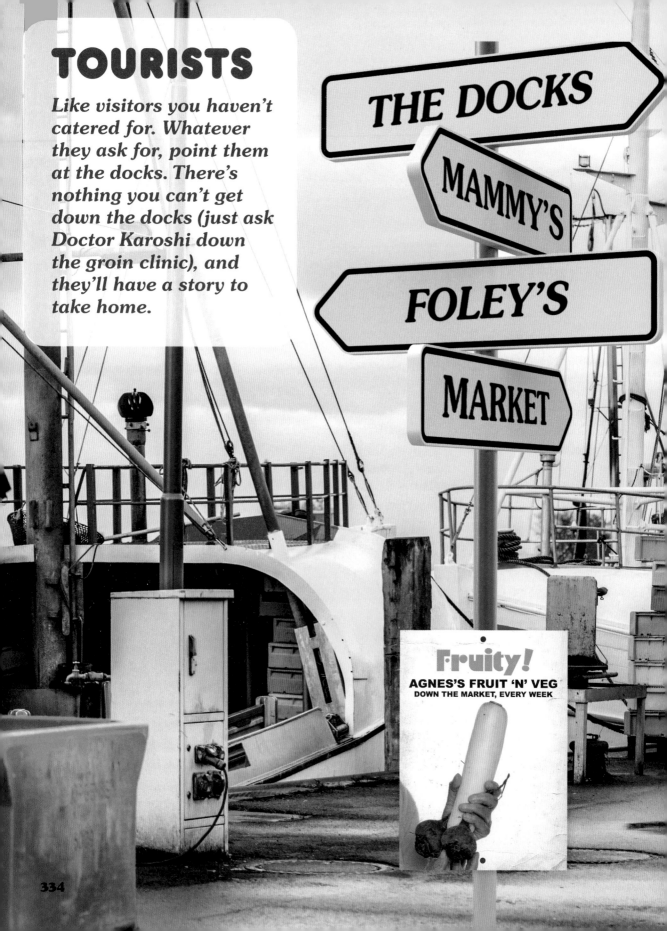

THE DOCKS

MAMMY'S

FOLEY'S

MARKET

Fruity!
AGNES'S FRUIT 'N' VEG
DOWN THE MARKET, EVERY WEEK

TRAINS

The train was invented by Robert Louis Stevenson in the good old days.

The first trains were steam trains, which is probably why there aren't many of them left. Metal ones came next, and they did last. You can see them now in museums, and next to a man with muttonchops and a whistle before a detective gets out and the murders kick off on the repeat channels.

Trains used to have three different levels of travel:

First Class

For uppity sods who can't travel without anti-maracas over the back of the seats. Free tea. Champagne bucket. Butler service. Enough space to stash your feckin' pony.

Second Class

For office workers and people who read big newspapers. Fabric-covered seats and luggage racks for leaving your baggage/the nippers on. Windows that open but don't necessarily shut.

SECOND CLASS

Third Class

For normal people. Wooden seats with splinters, not enough room to unwrap your egg sandwiches from their greaseproof paper, no roof, and an outside toilet. Real travel the way God intended.

These days, the normal people and the office people share the same carriage, but they kept the First Class ones, didn't they, so the Hilliary Nicholsons of this world can splash out extra money to pretend they're something feckin' special. But I've peeped in, and you're not missing anything: all they've got left is the anti-maracas. Turned out you can take money off idiots if they know there's something to stop their hair touching a public seat and a door between them and the rest of us. You could sell the eejits a sandpaper dildo if you told them the rest of us couldn't have one.

Trains are a great way to get to see the countryside. And also men's groins.

Unbelievable, they are, sprawled all over two seats with their legs spread wider than a doxy when the fleet's in, making it so you can't sit down next to them. The DART's got more crotches up for inspection than an STD clinic. I don't know what they're trying to tell me they've got down their pants, that sort of man, but they don't like it squashed. Sometimes I swing my handbag a bit wide as I go past, as a warning shot, to let them know it's better to keep it protected. Public service, that is.

The nippers get awful bored on trains, so they do. If you're travelling with your chisellers, make sure there's something for them to do. Like shout. Especially if you need more space.

Shouting kiddies are the perfect way of getting a few extra seats to put your legs up on. So is a strategically deployed hard-boiled egg. You start shelling one of those on the little table and people will go running like you just sprayed anthrax round the carriage.

TRAMPOLINES

When I was a nipper, the only place you saw a trampoline was at the circus. Now, when I look out of me back window, hasn't every kid in the neighbourhood got one in their garden?

When did this happen?

In my day, if you wanted to bounce, you did it on the bed. And then you were told to stop doing it on the bed. And then you stopped. And that was a valuable life lesson that sometimes you can just feckin' stop enjoying yourself and go and stare out the window.

Kids today don't even stare out the window any more. The closest they get is staring at their phones. They've digitalized feckin' everything.

I can understand the phones. Everyone's got a phone they're staring at now. I think it's nice. It means you bump into complete strangers. Quite a lot. And it's a sight for sore eyes when the odd gobshite falls down a manhole.

But the trampolines? Who decided that bouncing was a life skill you shouldn't stop a nipper from practising? We're raising a generation of feckin' Tiggers.

TWISTER

I'd forgotten all about Twister till a little while back, but every time I pick up a paper or a magazine, they're going on about how some celebrity's said something or other indiscreet on Twister. So I can only think getting tied up on a mat is all the rage again, them big stars out in Hollywood tangled in a big knot, gossiping to each other, thinking nobody can hear, but that's the whole point. You're all tangled up together, ear to mimsy, bum to tit. It's going to get out.

And make no mistake: Twister is filthy. I'm surprised there's not one of them papal bulls about it. It's exactly the kind of thing that usually gets Himself cheesed off.

There was only one way of getting smutty at parties when I was a young thing, and that was sardines. All crushed in a cupboard, the big fellas rubbing up against the girls. Still makes my knees go weak. Mind you, they're pretty feckin' weak already. They've got a combined age of about 140. (Can you still go weak at the knees if you get them replaced by artificial ones? I might have to ask Dr Flynn. If not, I'm keeping this pair, however wobbly they are. I wouldn't miss that sensation for all the tea in Superquinn.)

Anyway, there's no need for anyone to sweat in a cupboard now (unless you fancy that sort of thing) because the Good Lord, in all his wisdom, gave us Twister. The game where you get to do everything except actually putting it in.

God, it's porno-feckin'-graphic. And tree-feckin'-mendous. If your joints are up to it. Though I'd advise against playing it outside, in case the wind changes and you end up permanently stuck with your ankles behind your head. Round here, that's the sort of thing that can get you a shocking reputation. And a feckin' good nickname.

It's a wonder Twister isn't used more in hospitals. Christ, some of the positions I've been stirruped into as part of a routine inspection would bring tears to a contortionist's eyes. At least with Twister there you'd stand a chance of winning when someone laid their hand on a red spot.

(Winnie reckons she's got a foolproof way of fixing a game of Twister. Something to do with putting chewing gum on the spinning arrow. She says she once used it to get stuck for ages between two magnificent arses. I told her: now you know how that James May fella off *Top Gear* feels.)

Nothing but
UMBRELLAS

UMBRELLAS

It rains 225 days a year on average in some parts of Ireland. Usually the part where I'm standing. I don't get my hair done every two weeks to end up looking like a drowned cat, so I rely on a sensible rain hat, which I keep in my handbag when it's not raining, which is basically feckin' never.

Umbrellas are like rain hats, but especially large rain hats that blow inside out and only work properly when there's no wind. In other words, when there's no weather (see Weather).

Once an umbrella's blown inside out once, it will never be the same again. It's like trying to fix a bubble. Straight in the bin it goes, until the wind blows it out and it can flap about the streets like a stunned bat.

They say it's proper bad luck to put up an umbrella indoors. And so it is. They can shred a lampshade if you're not careful, and you can easily get stuck in the cupboard under the stairs for up to 24 hours (don't ask).

Mind you, it's feckin' pointless putting an umbrella up outdoors. They're the most useless invention since the revolving door. And trying to get through a revolving door with an umbrella is like trying to thread a needle with a sausage. Jaysus, I'm getting one of my heads just thinking about it.

If you want an umbrella – and God knows why you would – there are two types. One costs about €1 from every shop there is. The other costs about €40 and has a name like The Cavalier or The Plimsoll or The La-Di-Da Feckin' Winchester. Doesn't matter which one you buy, they all turn inside out as soon as there's a gust. Rubbish, the lot of them. You choose how much you pay for something that's going to last about ten minutes.

Feckin' cold

Feckin' cold

Feckin' cold

⚠ **WEATHER WARNING: Floods and broken umbrellas for weeks ahead**

IS FOR...

VIRUSES

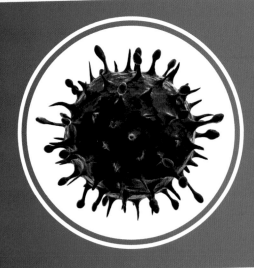

Viruses are tiny infectious monsters, even smaller than Rice Krispies, that are transmitted from human to human by sending the smaller human to school. My lot dragged home everything short of beri beri and gave it to me, the contagious little feckers. It was an endless cycle. I'd barely stopped sneezing when another chiseller trailed home with a nose like a smashed raspberry and a sleeve like a snail farm.

By the time I'd put half a dozen of them through school, my immune system looked like it had done ten rounds with Barry McGuigan. I swear there are more infectious diseases going round the average classroom than there were in the huts on the River Kwai. It's like the nippers brung home new diseases for me to try out. 'How's this, Mammy? It's slapped cheek syndrome. It's Welsh measles. It's a new flavour of flu.'

'Viruses' is the new name they have for bugs. 'Bugs', on the other hand, is what they now call insects. And 'insects' is unlawful relations between lawful relations.

But when I got a bug, I'd drag meself out of bed every morning, half-six sharp, no matter how much I ached, no matter how much I wanted to hide, and I'd carry on. There's no rest for a Mammy. Who's going to look after the family if you don't? If I'd left it up to Redser to make the nippers' porridge in the morning, he'd have waited until ten o'clock when the library opened before getting down there to look up the recipe. And even then, he couldn't have read the feckin' thing and would have torn out the pictures to copy.

No. You took the job on; they're depending on you.

And every morning I was up, no matter how poorly, packing the kids off to school and doing a day on the stall, then back to cook them their tea, and Redser's tea, and tuck them into bed, before safely packing Redser off down the pub for the night. And then, and *only then*, did I ever let myself feel ill.

That's what a virus means to a Mammy. Nothing. I may have had more hankies up my sleeve than Paul feckin' Daniels, but nobody saw me sneeze any more than anyone saw me shit. A Mammy is not weak, or the family will crumble. A Mammy is the keystone that holds the family arch. Which is why my head's that shape.

Men, on the other hand. Feck me. The fuss they make. The moaning, the complaining, the lying in bed with the curtains drawn. I'd call it 'man flu', but they're hardly men, more little sickly kittens with stubble and pyjamas. I remember Trevor coming back from Africa with these skin lesions and this 8-foot-long arse worm. The fuss he made! I told him I'd just got over a two-day sore throat and managed to make beans on toast for six, so he could come groaning to me when he'd done the same.

Just when you think you've had all the dise you can possibly have, they invent new on I've heard they've even got computer viruse which is why I always wear rubber gloves w I'm on Cathy's tablet. You can't be too care

VOLCANOES

Everything you need to know

Facts that will blow your mind

VOLCANOES

When Earth was growing up, it was covered in volcanoes. I've seen diagrams, and it looks like planet-acne. Ugly red lumps that get hot and angry until they pop out great gobs of nasty goo. (Mark had it terrible. I swear at one point I saw him put on a tight t-shirt and heard everything pop on the way through like someone putting bubble-wrap through a cardboard tube.)

The planet's grown out of its pimples now and, like most of us, the Earth only gets a really serious volcano these days when it's stressed out or has eaten a whole box of Celebrations.

Below: *Irritated pimple*

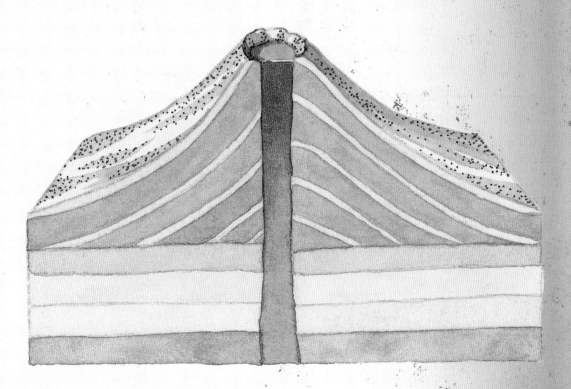

VOLCANOES

In Latin Times, the Roman city of Popeye was buried by a volcano, and all the people who lived there were turned into statues. And not good ones either, on a horse, or holding up a sword. Lying-down statues, all curled in a ball, refusing to get up. It looks like a whole city of teenage Dermots. Nobody wants to remember a civilization like that. No wonder they're not in charge any more. They look like a load of ancient layabouts.

Cathy showed me her holiday photos of Italy once and you wouldn't believe that with all those big brains they had to invent counting with letters (not to mention the pizza, which I will mention because God knows they're value for money down Superquinn) they left the tops off all their buildings. Try and take shelter in one of those Colosseums or Parthenons, you deserve every faceful of flying lava you get. Feckin' crumbling idiots.

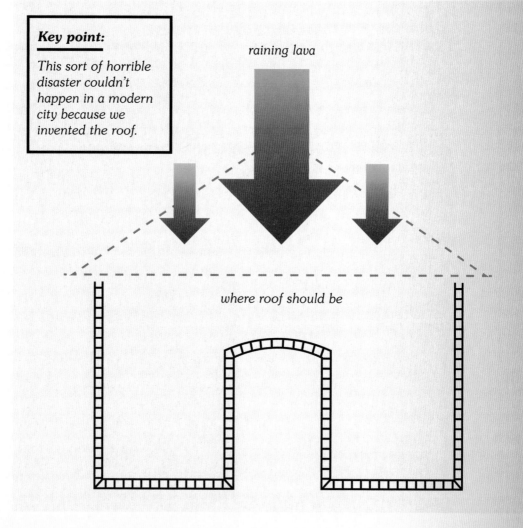

> **Key point:**
>
> *This sort of horrible disaster couldn't happen in a modern city because we invented the roof.*

raining lava

where roof should be

There was that volcano a few years ago that stopped everyone flying. Bliss, it was. For a few days there, it was like Ryanair didn't exist and that Michael O'Leary fella was just a bad dream. No being slapped for daring to have a bag. No being bollocked for wanting to go to the toilet. No being told to take your broken seat and shove it up your arse while drinking your €45 cup of tea like a man. It's just a shame there aren't more of that sort of volcano – the nice sort – now and then. That one wasn't a pimple. More of a beauty spot.

V IS FOR...

WASHING-UP

What people don't realize is that washing-up is just like sex.

For a start, you're going to need a towel at some point.

What's more, you start with the cleaner stuff (glasses; kissing) and get dirtier and dirtier until you end up with the really filthy stuff (roasting trays; roasting).

Plus it's good to have something squirty on hand for the more stubborn stuff. And you need to lick the cream off everything first. And you should only do it in the bath if there's no alternative. That bit's important.

What was I talking about?

Oh, washing-up. That's it.

There's one golden rule for washing-up: if you do it as you go along, you can stay on top and it doesn't need to get dirty.

And, in that respect, it's a bit like sex.

Jaysus, if you don't have sex regularly, when you get down to it, you find it's proper filthy. I've found myself bent over with a rented provider screaming for things I never thought I'd need. And if I'd just done it as I went along, I'd have been happy with a quick going over and a sit for a while to dry.

What was I talking about again?

EASY
NOZZLE

FILTHY

*FOR THE EXTRA
DIRTY HOUSEWIFE*

WASPS

Bees and wasps belong to the same family of animals, they say. But you know how, in a human family, there's some people who work for a living and get the respect of others, and some people who drone around, doing feck all, bingeing on sugary shite, ruining picnics and hurting people for no reason with an enormous stinger that's poking out of their arse? Exactly. That. (Some of this comparison might work better than other parts, but you get the idea.)

Wasps are extra bees, when bees were quite enough, thank you. The Lord in His generosity gave us a spare animal, like the spare button you get in shirts that gets put in a baccy tin with all the other buttons so you don't know which one's which. We didn't ask for An Extra Bee. It's not any real use. But there you go. Ours not to reason why. He made the Purple-Headed Mountain. He made the River Running By. And then He made An Extra Bee.

God normally corrects His mistakes. He's got form in that area.

I'll give you good odds that, before the Ark, there were spare versions of every animal, like the wasp/bee thing, that were basically the same but feckin' pointless, and He wiped them out. There was probably a camel with fourteen humps, and a cow that gave earwax instead of milk, and a horse with a red-hot back, and a kangaroo with dozens of those pockets and a glass lion and an edible giraffe, and snails with beaks and cats with horns and fish with feathers and *Jaysus these painkillers are strong*. It's no wonder I can't concentrate down the bingo.

Anyway, He probably wisely drowned them, in His mercy, so the world could be more perfect. But He missed the wasp. And we have to deal with the consequences. Life's like that. Sometimes shit happens.

If you're stung by a wasp, and you will be (and it'll be God's fault, bless Him), the best thing to put on it is vinegar. This is because wasps like jam, and vinegar is the opposite of jam. Take it from me. That's how that works (see Opposites).

WEATHER, THE

If the sky is God's television, then the weather is what's on at the moment. And all the time, come to that.

And as you'd expect, it's usually shite. People all have different ways of telling what the weather's up to. And if you're planning a wedding or a nudist barbecue, it's handy to be prepared, so here are the ways of telling what the weather is, in descending order of how much feckin' use they are.

Looking out the feckin' window	Asking someone who's just come in from outside	Checking Grandma's old barometer in the hall
One of those little weather houses with a fella and a lady who pop out	Looking at clouds	Using the colour of the sky
Checking if cows are lying down	Waiting till your joints throb	Watching those gobshites on the television with the maps

The best way to predict rain is to look out the window. If you can see that you've recently come in from putting a wash out, it'll be raining before the kettle's boiled.

Most weather, apart from sun, which is caused by going outside in a jumper, is caused by clouds, so it's useful to know the different sorts.

I use the 'hair' system.

Black clouds are the youngest

Grey are the ones getting on a bit

And the white ones are rickety old dears on their last legs

Young clouds are more active, the old ones keep themselves to themselves. So if you see a black cloud, think of it as a baby: it's going to piss on everyone and everything and make a God-awful noise until it's got your attention.

In Ireland, there's a fair lot of rain, so I always make sure I know where my umbrella is: it's on the back seat of the bus. Where I feckin' left it. Never mind. It was no use anyway as soon as a breath of wind yawned in (see Umbrellas). After that, it was no better than a paper serviette in a feckin' gale.

And remember the poem:

Red sky in the morning,

Shepherds' warning.

Red sky at night,

If you've been on a hill all day talking to sheep, you'll believe any old shite.

So the weather is pretty much shite TV. Except you can't turn over. Or off, for that matter. It's like when they've got TVs in pubs and you're trying to enjoy your cider, but there's a feckin' noise coming from the corner. And it's usually some gobshite telling you what's happening in a football match without bothering to show you any of it. Like those eejits in pop-up shops who shout through a microphone at the poor Mammies on the pavement, telling them this bag contains €100 worth of nice-smelling goodies for only €10, and it turns out it's all shite they could have bought down the cash and carry.

Well, that's the weather. A load of noise that isn't worth the paper it isn't printed on. (Is it? Can you get the weather in the post?)

WEEING IN PUBLIC

It's not something any woman would do, but you see the men round town, of a closing time, spraying it everywhere like elephants at a feckin' waterhole. I think it's something animal. Pheremenomes, they call it. Marking their territory. I reckon it's only millions of years of evolution that stops a man pissing his side of the bed to stop you rolling over on to it.

It's harder for a lady to relieve herself in public, even if she wants to. Unless she's bought one of those Shewees they have nowadays, and though I've thought it might be handy when I'm trying to make it back from Foley's to the safety of my own loo, staggering through the streets at full pelt, like Usain Bolt with an orange between his knees, I wouldn't want to put one of those funnel things back in my bag afterwards. Not without a little sachet of silica gel. It'd leave your handbag like a chip shop mop.

I've been forced to leave what you might call a 'wet shadow' in public only three times in my life, thank the Lord, and each time I hope I've managed to do it with at least some dignity. Once, in a layby by a main road when we'd broken down, taking care to face away from the flow of traffic to avoid a pile-up.

Once, behind a concrete structure at Tramore when I'd drunk six tins of shandy on a day so hot, when I looked down, the evidence had turned to steam, so it barely counts.

And once, years ago, when I got fierce nervous onstage and did it behind one of the Wise Men. I don't know why I was so nervous, I was only meant to be operating the curtain. The other parents really had a go at me. I told them it was 'a wee in a manger', but they didn't see the joke. I think they lost their sense of humour when Mary slipped on her face and dropped the little baby Jesus in it.

TOILETS

WEIRD FILMS

I have seen some weird films in my time. Ones that make no feckin' sense at all.

You know what's a good film? *Norbit*. It's got Eddie Murphy in it and this fat woman who I've not seen in anything else, but she's funny as and is going to go far. Cathy said it's a man in a dress but I can't believe they'd resort to something that cheap for laughs, not in this day and age.

But I do like to know what's going on in a film. If I get lost, I'm not afraid to ask questions. 'Who's that?' 'What's he doing now?' 'Is that a submarine?' 'Where did she buy those shoes from?' 'When's this going to finish?' It drives Cathy mad, but it's not my fault they make the films so weird. I'll ask loudly and clearly for an explanation, and if Cathy can't help, I'll find the projectionist and demand some proper feckin' answers.

So you don't have to suffer them, here's a list of the weirdest films I've ever seen. I'll admit I do sometimes nod off in films if I'm confused, but that's no excuse for them not making sense. I think that if they bothered to think about that more, there'd be loads of films winning Oscars every year, rather than just a handful.

GREASE

A right feckin' oddball of a film. I must admit, I was doing the washing-up for the first part of this, and then I got distracted by some cobwebs that have made little strings round the fanlight and me thinking I'd only given that a proper going over with the long duster last week, but it's about these two teenagers who like rock-and-roll singing but have gone off each other, but then the blonde one gets some trousers that are so tight and black they make it look like she's balancing on a pair of liquorice pipes, but the greasy lad likes that, so that's all sorted then.

And they celebrate by getting themselves a magic car that flies. It actually flies, right up into the sky, and I'm thinking, 'This is some film we've got here now. A flying car, if you please.' And then, just when you think, 'I wonder what adventures they'll have,' the film stops.

Feckin' rubbish. If you've got a magic car, use it! I remember a film about a magic car that the kiddies loved when they were babbies. What was it called? Chitty something or other. We must have watched it hundreds of times. Ah! *Christine*, that was what it was called. Watch that instead.

E.T.

A proper weird film. This boy finds a little old man in his shed, then puts him in his wardrobe, then sends him into space. There's some business with a load of men turning the house into a laboratory, and a bike that goes to the moon. (Do all your weird films have flying vehicles in them?) Now, if they're thinking they went to the moon on a BMX, when they couldn't do it in a feckin' rocket (see Man on the Moon) they've got another think coming. Rubbish.

WEIRD RATING

★★★☆☆

THE COMMITMENTS

What were they thinking? This one's set in Dublin, but I've watched it three times and I can't understand what's going on at all. I was mainly watching to see if anyone I know was in it, because, you know, you'd think someone I know would turn up. Winnie's always out and about, I thought maybe she'd be in it, crossing the road or something. But no. Not a sign of her. Or Buster. Or Dermot. Or Mrs McReedy.

And then I started wondering, bugger them, *where am I?*. You think I'd be in it. I'm out and about enough, doing the charity shops and that. And I'm down the market all the time. So I thought maybe that was what the film would be about, and someone, maybe a detective,

would turn up and solve the mystery of my disappearance. But there were songs and this big lad who sweats a lot, and they never get down to the nitty-gritty of what's happened to me or any of the locals. It's like I wasn't even born. You go and see a film with that good a premise – where am I? – and they do sweet Fanny All with it. What a waste.

WEIRD RATING

THE BIRDS

Bloody weird film where a woman gets punished for keeping millet in her pocket. Rosalie Cogan who does physical jerks for the over-50s down St Osaph's got followed by a pigeon for three days because it thought she had some crusts in her handbag. It happens. Still, right weird.

WEIRD RATING

MAMMA MIA!

Now, this is a weird feckin' film. It's about this girl who's gone to an island to get hitched and she's all in bits because she doesn't know who her dad is and she's just started to sing, and I'm thinking, 'Ah, now it's getting going,' and then it goes shhh and the screen goes fuzzy for a bit and this 15-minute football match breaks out. And then Hercule Poirot turns up for a spell, and he's about to point at your man from *Downton Abbey* in a vintage car, before there's some horseracing and a load of clips of that weathergirl Dermot likes.

Then there's more fuzzy stuff and there's a big dance number with James Bond in some ludicrous trousers and it finishes.

I didn't understand any of it. And there was only half a song in it, and it's supposed to be a musical and all. Must be one of those artyhouse films that lad who Cathy saw for a bit (with the glasses and the beard but no moustache – weirdo) was into. I honestly haven't got a breeze what was going on, but it made them all a fortune, so somebody feckin' likes it. I don't understand people any more.

Mamma Mia!
(DO NOT TAPE
OVER)

Dermot's
Weather Girl
Clips (Tape 58)

WEIRD RATING

★★★★☆

**ROXCO TIM-MATIC-
HAIR CUTTING BASICS**

BECAUSE YOU'RE WORTH IT!

HAIRCUTTING BASICS

Weird film I found in the bin in Cathy's room.
Think it's a remake of *Hair*, but the story's all over
the place and I didn't like the characters at all.
There was quite a promising bit with a trimmer,
but even that didn't go anywhere spicy. Weird.

WEIRD RATING

★ ★ ★ ★ ?

WEIRD VEGETABLES

Potatoes, onions and cabbage. That's what vegetables were when I was growing up. On special occasions, we'd have all three. And when there was someone coming to the house me Mammy wanted to impress, we might get carrots. But not too often. First time I saw a carrot, I thought my eyes were on fire. That a vegetable could be that colour! It was like staring into the feckin' sun.

Then the supermarkets arrived, all shiny and clean and full of tins. And in one of those tins was something beautiful – something magical.

PEAS.

Oh my God! Peas. Whose feckin' brilliant idea were they? The first blue food. Sure, they went green later on, after market research, I think it was. It may even have been down our market. I remember a lad with a clipboard. It was probably that. Or gas boilers. Anyway, when they were invented, peas were blue. And they were feckin' marvellous.

I can remember where I was when I first had peas: I was sitting at the dinner table.

'Mammy, what are these?' I said. And she looked down at me, all the love in the world in her eyes, cocked her head to one side, put one hand tenderly on me shoulder and said, 'Agnes, love – they're peas.'

'But Mammy!' says little me. 'There's *so many* of them!'

'That's peas,' she said, and I swear I saw a wistful tear welling in the corner of her eye.

I'd never eaten so many of the same thing in me life. Think about it. How much of something do you get with your dinner? About a quarter of a cabbage. Maybe a couple of potatoes. One tiny bit of a bit of a pig. But peas? Peas? Feckin' hundreds of them. You try to have hundreds of potatoes and you can't walk. And if you did what I did as a nipper, and ate your peas one by one, chasing them round your plate with the prong of your fork, stabbing at them like an Eskimo hunting a seal, you could be sat at that table for hours.

But it turns out peas were just the beginning.

All sorts of new vegetables started creeping into the supermarket. First it was broccoli, a funny-looking fecker which you could never cook for the right length of time. Always as tough as a dog-chew or as soft as wet toilet paper. Curly on top, then straight up and down, like a little vegetable Art Garfunkel.

Then along came peppers. Didn't I think pepper was a powder that comes in a little jar? Turns out it's made from these great big red and green fists with nothing inside them but little yellow dots. That's a wasteful vegetable right there. I thought you threw away lots with an onion, but Jaysus. I tried making stuffed peppers once and I couldn't split those little yellow things wide enough to get the rice in.

And then – God have mercy on us – a little super-powered stink bomb arrived from (where else?) France. Garlic. That little bastard. Impossible to get into without a hammer. And if you do manage to get into it, your fingers, your knife, your chopping board, your clothes and your kids will stink like Sacha Distel's hanky for the next six weeks.

One time, I tried making one of them chilli con carnivals, and I followed the recipe out of a magazine to the letter. 'Four cloves of garlic,' it said. How was I meant to know what a feckin' clove was? I thought the whole thing was a clove. Like it was French for 'stink bomb'. Four of those evil little bollixes I put in that pot. Jaysus, the morning after I had to belly-crawl along the landing to keep me poor head out of the noxious fumes. I didn't dare light a cigarette. The whole place would have gone up like a fireworks factory.

Garlic was just the start. Once they'd tricked us into thinking putting little time bombs full of bad breath into a perfectly normal casserole was acceptable, all sort of stuff with French names was sneaking its way into the shops.

Courgettes! mucky, soggy things. Like a marrow, but smaller and more expensive. Good for nothing. Imagine a child's green sock filled with mushy peas, but nowhere near as nice as that sounds.

Mange tout! like little beans that have been run over. Boil them for more than two minutes and they turn to snot. Dreadful business.

Celeriac! like celery but worse, if you can believe that. Which eejit thought, 'I know. Celery's horrible – let's make it more like a turnip'? Them mad scientists have a lot to answer for if you ask me. Disgraceful.

And once we'd got used to French names, along came the Chinese ones. Pak choi. Bok choi. La La. And Po. Or were they the Teletubbies? Well, I'm as likely to put one of them in a stew as a feckin' Teletubby, so it's no serious difference.

Now, round about now, the supermarkets had obviously run out of new vegetables, so they decided to jazz up some old ones by doing them different colours. So suddenly you've got yellow tomatoes. Yellow. Now, I might have been asleep the morning it happened, but I don't remember anyone saying, 'Sure, aren't you fed up with tomatoes being boring old red? It's so feckin' predictable. What if we made them more like a sort of salad traffic light?' Yellow tomatoes. I ask you. Mind you, at least they taste like tomatoes. The green ones taste like Brussels sprouts full of limescale remover.

Then there was some purple cabbage that goes grey when it's cooked, so it ends up looking like you've served everyone a portion of boiled underpants. Someone was up all night on that one.

And cabbages started to come in hundreds of types. They had more sizes and shapes than Lego. Pointy ones, floppy ones, curly ones, miniature ones (fuck off – a Brussels sprout's a Brussels sprout, not a tiny cabbage), long thin ones – how much cabbage can the world need? It's only the colourful bits in bubble and squeak. It's not a meal on its own.

Lettuce is no better. Since when were there 45 sorts of lettuce? To my mind, a lettuce is a lettuce is a bucking lettuce. You take it out of your burger and put it in the lid of the box, and then you throw it away, as part of a healthy diet. But I looked down the aisle in the supermarket and there was miles of the stuff, all different, in bags. No, me neither. I never asked for lettuce in the first place. Though I imagine walking along the aisle looking for proper feckin' lettuce might count as one of your five exercises a day, or whatever it is they have now.

It got so they had to rename actual lettuce so you could tell it apart from the other lettuces. It's not a lettuce now – it's an ICEBERG. It's meant to be healthy, keep you alive, but a fine feckin' reassurance that is to anyone who's seen *Titanic*. Though it's very low in cholesterol, so I suppose they can honestly guarantee 'your heart will go on'. Though probably not as long as that Saline Dion woman makes that song. I've sat through shorter funerals.

When I looked at all these other lettuces – some of them aren't even balls. A lettuce should be ball-shaped, that's the shape of a lettuce. Don't feck with the system. I swear some of these things aren't even finished. Rocket. Jaysus, rocket. It's just a load of weeds. That's not a lettuce, any more than a handful of scrapings off the hairdresser's floor is a feckin' rope. Plus it tastes like you shouldn't eat it. It's like stroking your tongue with peppered string. And I'm sure that's Mother Nature's way of telling you something. Probably that you shouldn't eat it.

But in the interests of research, I bought a basket full of these newfangled bags of modern lettuce. They turned out to mainly be newfangled bags of modern air, and that right there's a scam I'll be writing in to *Woman's Way* about as soon as I can be arsed. Here's what I found inside.

Radicchio: bitter as Hilliary.

Hearts of Romaine: named after a football team, and tastes like you're eating their away kit.

Endive: French. Not having it.

Lollo rosso: like a mouthful of crêpe paper Christmas decoration.

Spinach! apparently that's a lettuce now. Well whoop-de-do. There go the goalposts again.

Frisée! sounds like a haircut, tastes no better.

The next one I remember coming along was bean sprouts. Now, these little bastards arrived by stealth – in our Chinese takeaways. I never minded them when I hadn't spotted them. I didn't even mind them when I did spot them, because I thought they were crunchy little extra different noodles to go with the ordinary noodles. Then our Cathy goes on a feckin' diet and buys a packet of them one day, and Soppy Bollix here ends up cooking them. What an almighty rip-off! They're like little elastic bands made of water and feck all. No taste, no texture, nothing. She might as well have bought a bag of hand-reared, locally sourced, organic fresh air. Maybe that's what you're meant to do with all that puff you don't eat from a bag of supermarket salad: boil it up and make fresh-air soup.

Then, just when you weren't expecting it, along came fennel, which looked like a human heart and tasted like a Fisherman's Friend. As my Auntie Mini said after her honeymoon, 'There are some things you only put in your mouth once.'

Fennel =

Next up: the squash. Not 'squash', but *the* squash'. (Squash is orange juice for nippers, don't get them mixed up: the squash won't go up a straw.) *The* squash is some kind of mutant pumpkin beamed down from the planet Pain in the Arse that you have to cut in half with a knife about the size of a guillotine blade and then spend hours scooping all the seeds and bogeys out of. Not only is it a feckin' faff, it can kill you. And after all that, you have to roast the bastard. It'd be quicker to find and prepare a whole giraffe.

The first squash had a cutesy name: the butternut squash. Cheeky little fecker. I thought it might taste of butterscotch, so I went and bought one. Only when I got it home and realized I had something the size, weight and toughness of a fire extinguisher did I find out I'd been taken for a ride.

But now I go round the veg aisle at the supermarket, and the squashes have set up some sort of club that any giant vegetable can join. There's round green ones, long yellow ones, ones that are obviously pumpkins – I'm no fool – and ones that have feckin' flowers coming out of them.

I'm not eating any of this nonsense.

And lately, the new thing is vegetables you haven't got a clue about. You don't know their names and you wouldn't know how to cook them if the recipe was written on the side. I've seen all of this, and I had my reading glasses on, so I know I'm not making it up.

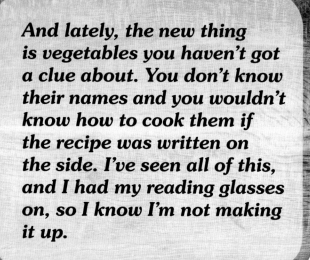

MOOLI

I mean, who came up with that? No one's going to buy something called mooli.

PAGE 3

Mammy's Dictionary

Okra: not even a real word.

SAMPHIRE:

sounds like she should have her knockers out in the paper.

Girolle: French. *Again.*

Sugar snap: you're not fooling Mammy. I bet there's buck all sugar in it.

ABBA

Edamame: I can't even pronounce that one. I think it's named after an ABBA song.

Shiitake: well, pardon me if that one doesn't speak for itself. And in a family supermarket, too. Fuckin' disgraceful.

If I were you, I'd stick to potatoes, onions and cabbage. And by that I don't mean purple potatoes, shallots and pointy cabbage that looks like it's a baddie from a puppet film – I mean proper potatoes, onion-shaped onions and normal cabbage. The dinner table is no place for running experiments on your family. (That's Grandad's armchair, while he's asleep.)

385

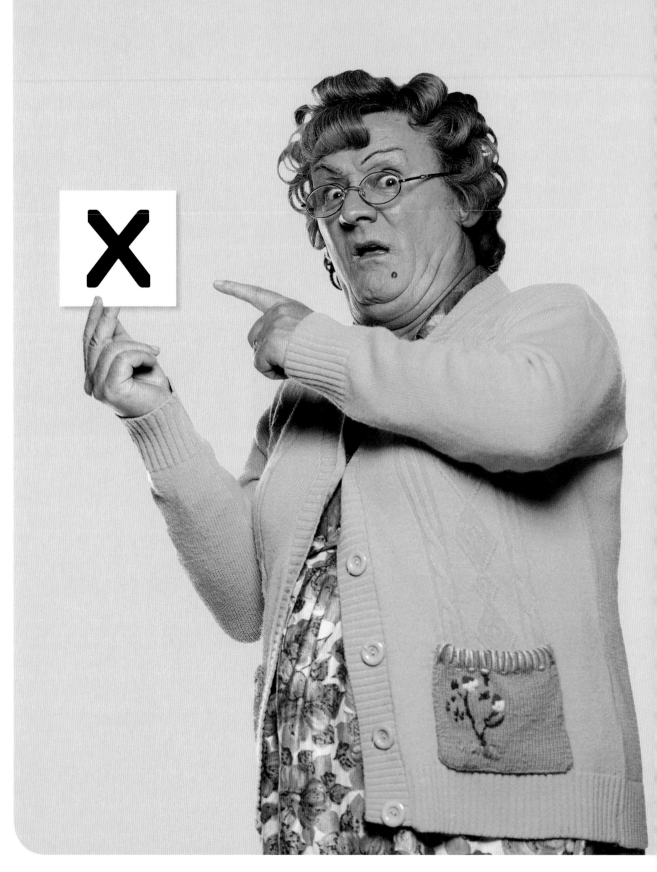

IS FOR...

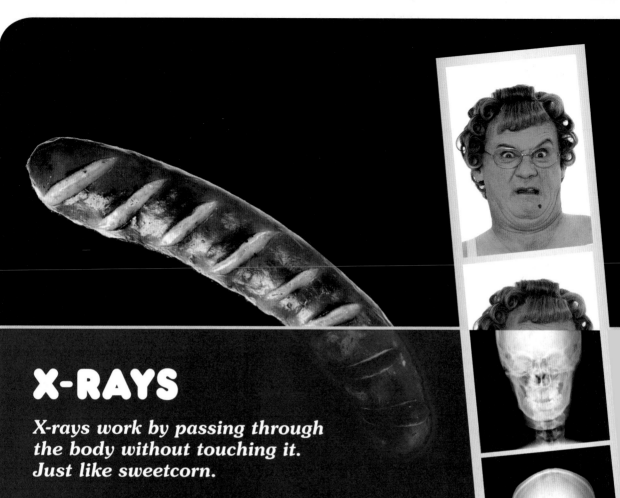

X-RAYS

X-rays work by passing through the body without touching it. Just like sweetcorn.

X-ray cameras remove all the flesh from the body, so are very flattering if you've suffered slight middle-aged spread related to, say, an allergic bloating reaction to excess Christmas pudding and want to look your best in a passport photo.

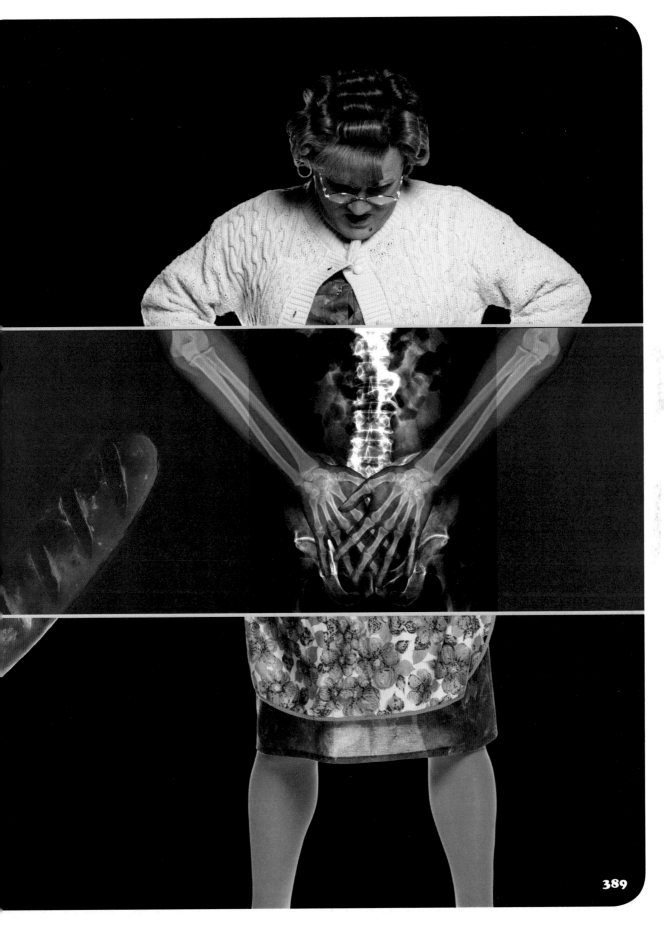

IS FOR...

YOGHURT

Yoghurt is off milk, and whoever thought of a way to sell that was some sort of feckin' genius. I bet some canny fecker's tried putting a load of strawberries in rank chicken and flogging that as a health food too. 'It really cleans your system out.' Damn feckin' right it does, like a sluice. The best flavour for putting on thrush is black cherry.

Mrs B's Spotted Strawberry Chicken Delight £45.99!

IS FOR...

...FECK ALL.

NOTHING BEGINS WITH Z.

This book didn't just write itself out of my head. I had to research it properly from other places, because I was told to. It's fierce hard, because apparently you're not allowed to just copy bits down off the Wikimajaysewhat (which is what ruined Dermot's homework-writing service) so I've taken what I found out other

places and put it in my own words. Which is handy, because I didn't believe a word of most of it. I don't know where these book-writing fellas get their so-called facts but they could do with living a few years in the real world like me.

BIBLIOGRAPHY

Wikimathingumajig – by loads of internet weirdos (Cathy's tablet pad thing)

Manual for Zanussi ZWG6120K washing machine – by Zanussi (Zanussi)

Manual for Creda 17021 washing machine – by Hotpoint (Hotpoint)

Manual for Bosch WAQ28461GB washing machine – by Bosch (Bosch)

Manual for Siemens WM14Y791GB washing machine – by Siemens (Siemens)

Indesit Guide to Drain Pump Cleaning – by Indesit (Indesit)

Indesit IWB71250 – by Indesit (Indesit)

Great Big Book About Goats – by a goat-expert fella (library)

Great Big Book About Aeroplanes – by some pilot or other (library)

Great Big Book About Nucular Reactors – by some boffin or other (library)

Great Big Book About Maps – by the map people (library)

Great Big Book About Spiders – by a spider expert (library)

Great Big Book About Great Big Books – by some book expert (library)

Budgie The Little Helicopter – HRH Duchess of York (Barnardo's shop)

Reader's Digest Family Book of Knowledge – Reader's Digest (Bird Rescue Service shop)

Guinness Book of Amazing Insect Records – Norris McWhirter (Barnardo's shop)

Daily Mirror Book of Facts – Toxteth O'Grady (Goodwill shop)

Ladybird Book of Vikings – Stephanie Barton (Oxfam shop)

Well, I Never Knew That About Sausages – Irish Meat Marketing Board (leaflet from D. Flaherty, family butcher's)

Teach Yourself Grade 6 Clarinet – Adrienne Postgate (church jumble sale)

Our Friend Creosote – Haningfield Scientific Press (Goodwill shop)

Train Your Tortoise the Meeten Way – T. Meeten (Barnardo's shop)

Essentials of Meat Storage: Expiration Dates – Castlereagh Borough Council (Oxfam shop)

You Can Beat Your Simon: How to Win at the New Electronic Games – Gavin Weeds (Enable Ireland shop)

Win the Lotto: Strategies for Success – Dr K. Orvelsson (Goodwill shop)

To The Best Mum In The World – Clinton Cards (Oxfam shop)

Cooking with Salad Cream: 401 Recipes – Jeroen V. Gustavus (Vincent's shop)

The Smurfs Learn About Continental Drift – Bo Owls (Irish Cancer Society shop)

She Tamed the Cockle Man – Llewellina Nubelle (Sue Ryder shop)

Linoleum Layer of Hearts – Davinia Poods (Enable Ireland shop)

Succumb to the Wharfinger – Clara Kindavid (Barnardo's shop)

399

Acknowledgements

Thank you to Graeme Hunter for the photography, to Helen Cannon and Nicole Tulloch for make-up, to Jenn Foord for the props, to Melbourne Convention Centre, to Tim Lewis and Tabasum Patel at Unreal for their design work, to Jason Hazeley and Joel Morris for the words, to Tim Broughton, Katie Sheldrake, Emma Brown, Fiona Crosby, Lee Motley, Dan `Ginger Balls´ Bunyard and Anna Derkacz at Penguin, to Conor Gibney, Dean Donnelly, Gareth Woods, Derek Reddin, Marian O´Sullivan and Mark Sheridan for their assistance on the day, to Helen Spain and Emily Regan for costumes, and to Fiona Gibney for brilliantly organizing everything and making it all run smoothly.